Marianna Shore

A Rainbow, An Acorn, and Four Children

Bumblebee Books
London

BUMBLEBEE PAPERBACK EDITION

Copyright © Marianna Shore 2024

The right of Marianna Shore to be identified as author of this work has been asserted in accordance with sections 77 and 78 of the Copyright, Designs and Patents Act 1988.

All Rights Reserved

No reproduction, copy or transmission of this publication may be made without written permission.
No paragraph of this publication may be reproduced, copied or transmitted save with the written permission of the publisher, or in accordance with the provisions of the Copyright Act 1956 (as amended).

Any person who commits any unauthorised act in relation to this publication may be liable to criminal prosecution and civil claims for damage.

A CIP catalogue record for this title is available from the British Library.

ISBN: 978-1-83934-944-7

Bumblebee Books is an imprint of
Olympia Publishers.

First Published in 2024

Bumblebee Books
Tallis House
2 Tallis Street
London
EC4Y 0AB

Printed in Great Britain
www.olympiapublishers.com

Dedication

To the reader of this book: I hope this novel brings you to exciting places, where these four children went to, and are able to learn to explore new and exciting experiences and places.

1 THE MERRIFIELD PRIMARY SCHOOL
2 THE SCHOOL BELL
3 SAMMY AND ROLAND HAVE A RACE TOGETHER.
4 THE SILVERTON CHILDREN ARE GOING HOME FROM SCHOOL.
5 THE SILVERTON FAMILY GET TOGETHER.
6 ROLAND HAS A BIRTHDAY PARTY.
7 SAMMY AND SALLY PLAY IN THE GREEN MEADOW PARK.
8 THE SILVERTONS GO TO TEA WITH THE BROOME FAMILY.
9 THE RAINBOW CAKE.
10 THE CONFESSION.
11 THE UNEXPECTED PHONE CALL
12 A NEW START FOR THE BROOME FAMILY
13 AN ACORN, A RAINBOW, AND A BABY OAK TREE
14 MR QUICK THE BANK MANAGER

CHAPTER 1
THE MERRIFIELD PRIMARY SCHOOL

Mrs Saunders the Headmistress, of The Merrifield Primary School, and her secretary Miss Bracket are both inside Mrs Saunders's office. Mrs Saunders is pacing up and down the room, worrying about her school, she feels a need for some fresh air to clear her mind, so she walks across the room, to the sash window, lifting the window up, for some fresh air, and takes a deep breath of cool air coming in.

'Hmm, lovely fresh air, she murmured, still thinking about her school, and wondering how the children were settling in, and if the teachers, were happy with their pupils?

Her eyes suddenly gaze down to Jeff the caretaker, who is watering the Hydrangeas, which are growing in large tubs, just outside the school window's building, with his faithful old green watering can. Apart from the pink and blue hydrangeas, Mrs Saunders is admiring also, alongside the flower beds, are giant yellow, and small red Sunflowers, which some of the older children, have planted the sunflower seeds in pots earlier in the year, the yellow sunflowers are growing tall, with they have large yellow wide flower heads, the plants are against near the wall of the school building the red sunflowers, are smaller and daintier, next to the tall yellow sunflower ones. In the distance fields, she hears a quiet hum, and wonders where the noise is coming from.

She spots out there in the yonder field is a farmer, ploughing his tractor, which he is steering.

His green and grey tractor up and down his field, the tractor is turning the earth over, ready for the next crop of seed potatoes to be planted there.

Mrs Saunders's eyes suddenly, look back to Jeff, he feels someone watching him, he looks all around, and glimpses at Mrs Saunders peering down at him, from her window, he smiles, and waves to her, she smiles back, and quickly turns around, back to Miss Bracket, who is still reading out loud a letter, to herself, not knowing, she was being heard by Mrs Saunders, her eyes head back down to Jeff again, and realised that she did not wave to Jeff, but Jeff has now left from watering the flowers, and heading back to his shed, to tidy up, before getting ready to go home.

Miss Bracket, who is now sitting down, at her faithful old typewriter, typing frantically away. trying to get her typing done, before she rushes off, to make a much-needed cup of tea, as she is very thirsty, after having a salty bacon breakfast, that morning.

Mrs Saunders mentioned to Miss Brackett who is still typing on her typewriter.

'I was looking at the garden here just now, and admiring how colourful the garden, is, despite the time of year.'

Miss Bracket stops typing, and looks up, and smiles

at Mrs Saunders, and replies back to her.

'Yes, I love this time of year, very soon the leaves will be turning yellow, orange, and golden brown, very beautiful. I love walking in the woods, with the wet ground wafting, a lovely fresh smell of damp leaves, the Autumn is magical, the gentle breeze, blowing through my hair, and on the ground are laden with horse chestnuts, we would find conkers, with their, beautiful sheen brown colour, they mimic shiny oak wood, and as a child, we would gather up the conkers, and bore a hole in the middle of the conker, thread a string through it, tie a knot, and have a conker match, with our friends, and try to hit the conker off, the opponents string, as we swing, it onto the opponent conkers, while they hold it still, making sure they keep it away from their face, then hitting the conker, the one with the conker still, on the string is the winner!!

Also, when the leaves fall off the trees, this time of year, I used to love to run under the tree, and try, and catch the leaves before they landed, on the ground, what happy days, we had in those times, do children play with conkers these days, I wonder? Children are so different, maybe I am old fashion about the good times, I am sure they do not enjoy the pleasures we used to have. Said Miss Brackett reminiscing.

'I agree Miss Bracket, life was so simple and kind, what were you were saying about a parent request just now,' enquired Mrs Saunders, who was now bored with all this talk about Autumn.

'I did not realise that I was reading this letter out loud just now, but in this letter, Mrs Bonneville inquires, can we take her twins girls soon, possibly next week,' asked Miss Bracket, looking at Mrs Saunders for her reply.

Mrs Saunders replied, 'Maybe, what did she say about the children ages were Miss Brackett?

She realises she needs to shut the window, as she is talking about a parent and her children and she thinks now, she needs to talk without anyone else hearing her conversation, as there is a need for confidentiality now requires. The window is now shut tight.

Mrs Saunders is now facing Miss Brackett, who has now started reading the letter, out loud to her again.

Miss Brackett looked down at the letter to find the children's ages.

'Ah here it is seven years old,' she said, sliding her finger down the letter, at the appropriate place.

'Yes, we could possibly manage to do that, they would go in Mrs Gelder's class, with Patty the Nursery Assistant, the one who comes in the morning' informs Mrs Saunders, looking pleased about new children arriving.

Then adding 'please write back please Miss Brackett, and say yes, we will look forward to meeting, her two children, also can you describe the uniform details, and any other information needed.

Then Mrs Saunders, goes on to say, in fact, I need to see them, before they start, to make sure, they know the teachers, and other information, about the school information.

Can you add in the letter, if they could come on Wednesday, the fourteen of September, that will give them time, to receive this letter, and buy the uniform, they can start on the same day, if they are happy with the School, and their form teacher, Miss Gelder. If they wish we can show them, a few class- rooms, before they start,' said Mrs Saunders.

'I am looking forward to having the twins, they are either different, to look at, or maybe have completely, other personality traits, the last set of twins we had were so different, one had black hair, the other had blond hair' said Miss Brackett.

'Thank you, Miss Brackett, I am aware of twins, we have two adorable twins, in my road, girls twins, Lily and Poppy, they are only two years old, but they have a long time, before starting school, they will probably go to this school, when they are older, the twin's mum Zoe, is a working mum, her own Mother the children's granny who name I believe is Lydia, looks after the twins, while mum is at work, Lydia, is a lovely lady, a retired Midwife, she quite used to children, and her knowledge of health, which is very important to her, as well as her own professional skills.

'Brilliant,' said Miss Brackett, smiling at the thought of new children, coming to this school, adding, 'When I have finished this letter, I will go, and make, you a cup of tea, with two spoons of sugar, and some biscuits, whatever I can find in the staff room biscuits tin'

'Excellent, said Mrs Saunders, I have a Mrs Dankworth, coming this afternoon, Mrs Dankworth's child started last year, but she is having arithmetic problems, which she finds difficult, but we can soon remedy that, we have a new method of Arithmetic, coming soon which should solve the problem for Teresa.

After I have finished my tea, I need to see Mrs Coates, and hopefully, find her in the staff room.

But first I need to read some notes, from Miss Kelly. who gave me, some useful information about different physical exercises, for children, that they may enjoy, doing than the normal ones they do every week.' admits Mrs Saunders.

Miss Brackett stood up, and headed, for the staff room, she returned twenty minutes later, with a tray, that included, one cup of tea, one cup of coffee, and five assorted biscuits on a plate.

Miss Brackett puts down the tray, and hands Mrs Saunders a cup of tea, she held out the plate of biscuits, giving her a chance, to take what she wanted from the plate, Mrs Saunders reaches, out and takes two biscuits, from Miss Brackett's plate, as she is holding the plate out for her.

'Thank you, Miss Brackett who places the biscuits on her lap, and the tea on the table, beside her chair.

Miss Brackett takes the tray, with the coffee and biscuits, and rests the tray on the side table, and sits down on a soft chair.

'Ah! just what I needed,' admits Miss Brackett, lying back on her chair.

Mrs Saunders is sat on an upright foldaway chair, she feels happier, sitting in the upright chair, while still being in control of the situation.

'What a week,' moans Miss Brackett, sighing with relief after a sip of her coffee.

'Yes, I hope Mrs Dankworth is coming soon, I will fetch up her from the hall, and escort her to my office, after that. I need to ask for someone, to ring the bell, as soon as I finish this tea, and finish writing some notes out, you can pop along soon, when you have finished your coffee, thank goodness for Friday, we can look back at the new week, and hope the new children, have settled in, so we can have an easy term,' Mrs Saunders announces to Miss Brackett.

'Okie dookie, my cat will need feeding, when I get back,' admits Miss Brackett.

'Do not talk about cats to me, my cat Polly, has been such a worry to me, for several months, I nearly thought of taking her to the blue cross home for unwanted cats,' groaned Mrs Saunders, looking angrily at Miss Brackett for the cat word.

'I am sorry, I will not mention it again' whispers Miss Brackett nervously worried that she has upset Mrs Saunders.

Miss Brackett quickly picks up her handbag, and scuttles around, to get ready for a quick, get away from Mrs Saunders, as her comments about the cat word has obviously upset Mrs Saunders, so I must not say anymore cat words mentioned again.

'I will go now if that is aright, 'she asked nervously to Mrs Saunders.

'Bye Miss Brackett see you on Monday,' calls out Mrs Saunders.

Miss Brackett leaves the room and shuts the door quickly and quietly.

After Miss Brackett leaves the room, Mrs Saunders, then realised she must have upset Miss Brackett by her swift exit.

She sits back down on the chair, pondering, and hopes that Miss Brackett is okay.

Mrs Saunders then tidies away the book, she was writing in, and returns it back on the shelf, she looks arounds inspects the room, to make sure that the room is ready for any visitors coming, and moves a chair ready for Mrs Dankworth who will probably come without her husband, as he is not expected to come, Teresa her daughter is already in the school building, and will come up, with her mother, when she arrived in the hall, where Teresa will be waiting for her.

The rest of the children that attend the Primary school, in the country of Denton, in the county of Sunningdale, were getting ready to go home, this is a new team, of a new year, they have come back, after having a long summer break at home, and are keen to get back to School, and learn something new again, and see their friends, which they have not spoken to for several weeks.

Four friends, who attended Merrifield Primary School, are Sally and Sammy Silverwood, and Molly Broome, they are glad to go back to school, but not Roland Broome, Molly's brother, who is very not happy, to be coming back to school, he is not popular with his class mates, they say nasty words to him, and make rude comments about his size, and called him Rely poly, and porky.

This made Roland unable to socialise, with his classmates, so he hides himself away from them, Sammy had more patient, and he tried to help Roland, and told him to ignore their rude comments, from his classmates, Roland needed to be brave, and put on a strong front, now brags about his muscles, this upset the younger children, which was far from the truth, Roland, does not do any exercise, he only sits around at home, watching television, eating cakes, and biscuits, which did not give him, any muscles at all, his body, just got fatter, and fatter, which because of his weigh, makes his walking difficult to achieve at times.

Sammy was glad to get back to school, he was bored at home, he enjoyed learning, and loved his sports days, and competing in running races, and playing with his friends, he made his friends laugh, by imitating cartoon characters, he saw on the television.

Sally is more serious and quieter, like her Dad, Sally has two friends Hattie and Ellie.

Molly is more outgoing, and has a happier disposition, she has a slightly smaller frame, like her mother, but unfortunately Sammy takes after his father with a slightly bigger frame, both Sally and Molly, played with each other, when the two families, get together at the weekends.

Kathy and Wayne Broome are Roland and Molly's parents. Kathy had a difficult childhood, As her parents were always drinking, Kathy and her brother, Kenny had to fend for themselves, and they fed themselves on fried bacon and chips. Wayne Broome, who is Kathy's husband is also a drinker, because of this Kathy, found she was with someone who was familiar with her background, and whom she could relate to. Because of Kathy, having a difficult childhood, and was starved of affection, she only could give her children, lots of food, this was her way of showing, she loved them, and having any no knowledge, about healthy foods, she was very naïve, by giving them bigger portions of fatty foods, this was what Molly and Roland, got instead of any physical love and affection, she just gave them food, as a substitute for love, which was her only way she knew. But luckily for Roland and Molly they attended a good school, where they were given healthy school lunches, they had chips, but only once a month at school, but the Roland and Molly still had bad habits at home, they did not enjoy eating healthy food from school, they thought healthy food was boring and tasteless, and much preferred eating sweets, cakes and puddings, they did not like the taste of alcohol, as they both secretly tried alcohol, from the Fridge, and decided alcohol taste were too bitter, Roland and Molly preferred sweet lemonade, and fizzy drinks, that Kathy had brought them.

In their school, The Merryfield Primary school, Mrs Saunders who is the Headmistress, is an excellent headmistress, caring for her pupils as if they were her own, she has no children, or a husband anymore, so she devoted her time and energy, in running the school, Mrs Saunders gives the pupils, her time, patience, kindness, and understanding, and make sure that her school is running smoothly with- out any problems. They had regular staff meetings, to discuss the children's welfare and education, to suit their needs, also alongside Mrs Saunders, is Mrs Coates the deputy Headmistress, and several teachers, some cooking staff, one cleaner called Hattie, and a caretaker called Jeff, who looked after the school grounds, and their one large grass playground. The only concrete area, are where the staff and some parents, park their cars, safely out of the way away from the children playground.

Mrs Saunders the headmistress is heading to the staff room, to ask Mrs Coates the deputy headmistress a favour, but she met her first in the corridor.

Mrs Coates was also looking, for one of the teachers, about a new Maths method, to help pupils learn Maths in an easier way, and was heading to the staff room, to find a Mrs Coates who should be having a cup of coffee, and a break from her classroom.

'Ah ha, you are just the person, I was coming to ask you for a favour, could you ring the school bell for me today, I will be seeing a parent soon, so I need to be ready for her, I need to have my thoughts, ready for Mrs Dankworth, and have all the paper work in front of me,' informs, Mrs Saunders, to Mrs Coates.

'Fine, not a problem,' answered Mrs Coates.

'You could get a child, from Miss Potters class, if it the bell is not too heavy for them, to hold, 'asked Mrs Saunders.

'Yes, of course, what a good idea for some child, who would love an opportunity, to ring the school bell, I think Miss Potters' class would be the right age group to ring the bell,' replies Mrs Coates.

'Yes, good idea, thank you,' Mrs Coates, said, to a relieved Mrs Saunders, by the way, what do you think, about the cat book, I lent you, did it help your cat, and did you find it useful? I bought the book as I was having a problem, with my cat Tommy, he was waking me up, very early in the morning, meowing for food, the answer was very useful, I now give him a bigger meal, at night, and he is not so hungry in the morning, and I then give him his food, at eight o'clock in the morning, the same time as my breakfast time,' informs Mrs Saunders.

'I love cats too, and I found your book very interesting, and useful, and it has a lot of answers in it, and the photographs of the cats are very beautiful,' admired Mrs Coates, smiling.

'Yes, I love the photography in the book too, it has a good name title "How to understand your Moggy 'by Katherine Matthews,' replies Mrs Saunders.

'Did they have a series called, how to manage children,' asks Mrs Coates smiling.

'Hmm, we do need to be serious Mrs Coates, about our children, they are children not adults they are children learning about, our teaching staff are managing the children very well thank you Mrs Coates' said Mrs Saunders feeling very angry with Mrs Coates mentioning of her children here at her school.

'I am sorry, this is a serious subject, I am very worried about these children too, some are either too thin, or overweight, this is something, which will be brought up at the staff meeting next week,' said Mrs Coates apologising.

'There are some children, who are doing okay, and there are those we must watch, I am concerned about Roland,' whispered Mrs Coates.

'Do you mean Roland being overweight? and others who are under weight, and those who are showing their ribs, not good,' said a worried Mrs Saunders.

'No, I blame the parents, they overindulge their children, with greasy foods like bacon sandwiches, which they take to school and consume in the morning break, an hour before their lunch, which is far too much for a young child to absorb and digest, so early in the morning!!

'The thin children are a worry too, we had one child who fell asleep in Miss Copeland's class, snoring all the way through a History lesson,' confessed Mrs Coates.

'What did Miss Copeland do? enquires Mrs Saunders, upset about hearing that about this thin child sleeping in her classroom.

'She did nothing, but asked the child in question later, was she getting enough sleep', said Mrs Coates

What was her reply? asked Mrs Saunders.

'She just cried, and ran away,' said Mrs Coates, sadly.

'Oh, how what a shame, that should not happen, these days, that we still have underfed children, Mrs Coates, this is such a problem, as those who are overweight children,' admits Mrs Saunders sadly.

'Yes, I will discuss this matter next week, at the staff meeting I must go, I will put on my thinking cap, I wish it was that easy, we must keep thinking Mrs Coates,' said Mrs Saunders, looking and checking her watch, she gives it a gentle tap, my watch still isn't working well,

I must have it seen to. I must not be late for my talk with Mrs Dagworthy, I just need to make sure, I am not late for her, Mrs Dankworth's daughter is having a problem with her English homework and getting it ready on time, to give to her teacher' enquires Mrs Saunders.

'Sorry, Mrs Coates, you were saying, asked Mrs Saunders, upset for interruptions Mrs Coates.

'Why, yes, I have finished your book, my cat Bella, would scratch the furniture, it is now in threads, and ruined, your book also gave me some good tips or two, I have no idea that when a cat is angry with you, he puts his tail in the air, and moves it side by side, we learn sometimes new, every day don't we Mrs Saunders,' remarked Mrs Coates, said with a surprised look.

'What a lot of problems, our cats give us, 'Mrs Coates admits.

'Yes,' Laughs Mrs Saunders, nodding her head.

'I will bring your book, back next week, if that is okay, otherwise I could pop over on Saturday to your house, on the way, that I go to do my shopping, Mrs Saunders' replies to Mrs Coates.

'I can wait till next week, don't forget we have a meeting next week, with the staff, reminds Mrs Saunders.

'I will provide the cakes; Mrs Saunders' insists Mrs Coates.

A real treat, I am looking forward to enjoying your cakes again,' admitted Mrs Saunders, smiling, adding, 'Are you making your famous butterfly cakes,'

'Yes, I will put some crystallised ginger bits in it, I know you like your ginger, and I will add my usual Vanilla extracts,' says Mrs Coates.

'I love vanilla, it reminds me of having an ice cream at the seaside, I love strawberry and chocolate ice cream. I love to make my own ice-cream occasionally, in my new freezer,' admits Mrs Saunders.

'That reminds me, I must book my holidays, with my friends from my art classes, we are going to France this year, to paint the country scape sceneries, so we will need to get booking. these holidays are very popular, they not only teach people, who have never painted in their lives, but they are happy to have people, who are experience painters who like to dabble, and do their own free painting, of course, we like to help the new painters, which is nice, for them to see how we paint, and to paint their way in their own style,' informs Mrs Coates.

'How are you getting on, with your painting Mrs Coates? asks Mrs Saunders.

'I am trying out, with acrylic paintings this time, it is different from watercolour, I am hoping to attempt to paint a building, it is a challenge doing any painting,' admits Mrs Coates.

'I am more of a photographer person, if it does not always look right, but at least it is a clean hobby, see you next week, at the staff meeting, for a catchup on our children,' said Mrs Saunders reminding Mrs Coates.

'I do like your watch, Mrs Saunders,' admitted Mrs Coates, smiling.

'Thanks, my boyfriend bought it for my birthday, is but it is a good watch, but I believe it is not that expensive, my boyfriend has a knack, of buying good quality presents,' admitted Mrs Saunders, looking at her watch again.

'Thank you, again Mrs Coates, for the compliment, I hope you find a child, to ring the school bell,' says Mrs Saunders hopefully.

Mrs Saunders returned to her study, and Mrs Coates proceeds towards Miss Potters classroom.

CHAPTER 2
THE SCHOOL BELL

Mrs Coates strolled down the corridor towards Miss Potters classroom, and gently knocks on her door.

'Come in,' Miss Potter shouts.

Mrs Coates walks into the classroom, and sees Miss Potter, standing at the blackboard, she goes over to her.

Her class are all busy, writing down, from the black board, some difficult words, when a quiet hum echoes around the room, they stop their writing, and they look up and watch Mrs Coates, with wonderment of this interruption, which they do not see often.

'Can I borrow a child to help me, ring the school bell please,' she asked Miss Potter.

'Yes of course, what a good idea, I will ask the class, who would like to help you ring the school bell, I know some children will love to, and others may not, it is a heavy bell, it needs a strong hand, 'replies Miss Potter.

Miss Potter claps her hands, to make the children listen to what, she needs to say.

The children wait, to listen to what Miss Potter, has to say, and curious to wonder, why Mrs Coates has come into the room.

'Now children, who would like to ring the school bell for Mrs Coates,' asked Miss Potter, looking around the room.

Lots of hands quickly go up.

Miss Potter looks around the room, and sees Dominic's hand, go up, as lots of the children do too.

A lot of 'Me'! Miss Potter please, 'shouts the children around the room.

Dominic says nothing, but quietly waits, with his hand, still in the air, as with the rest of the children, doing the same.

Miss Potter thinks she would choose Dominic, as he is waiting, patiently.

'Right Dominic, you can go with Mrs Coates, and help her ring the bell, please,' smiles Miss.

Potter announces at the quiet Dominic, which has surprised him.

He gets up and goes, over to Mrs Coates.

'Thank you, Dominic, Miss Potters said, 'now go with Mrs Coates, Dominic, we will wait for you to come back, before heading home, so do not worry, your classroom, will not be empty before you return,' admits Miss Potter, hopefully reassuring Dominic.

Miss Potter knows that Dominic is a worrier, and he panics, at the smallest problem to be had.

Dominic stands next to Mrs Coates, who looks down at Dominic.

'Hello Dominic, would you like to ring the school bell with me,' asked Mrs Coates, just to make sure he can cope with this heavy school bell,' she smiles at Dominic, who now looked, maybe this is going to be, quite a problem for me.

Dominic nods.

Mrs Coates holds out her hand to Dominic, who slips his hand, into Mrs Coates hand.

She noticed that Dominic hands are cold, her warm hand, is very comforting for Dominic, who knows this adult, will be kind to him.

'Thank you, Miss Potter, said Mrs Coates.

Dominic and Mrs Coates, walk towards the door, and opens it, and they both proceeded down the corridor, towards the front door, on the way down the corridor, Mrs Coates stops.

'Dominic, I need to get the bell from the cupboard,' she said, she lets go of Dominic's hand, and opens a small cupboard, and takes out the large heavy bell, she shuts the cupboard, carries the bell, and the two of them walk, towards the door of the playground.

Mrs Coates, flings open the door, and holds the door open, so that they both can go outside safely.

Mrs Coats, and Dominic step outside, Mrs Coates is still carrying the heavy hand bell.

She looks down at Dominic, and asked, Dominic.

'Now, Dominic, she speaks quietly, to Dominic, 'are you able to hold this bell, and ring it loudly so, the whole of the school, can hear it.' Enquires Mrs Coates.

'Yes, Mrs Coates,' answers Dominic quietly.

She hands the bell to Dominic, and tells him, you will need two hands to hold it.

She places the bell, into Dominic's hands, he holds the hand bell, carefully, with both hands and lifts it in the air, clang the bell, it makes a loud noise, vibrating through the air, as it rings 's loudly, he continues, to make the bell clang, and, he keeps on going, after he has it, rung about seven times.

Mrs Coates asked Dominic to stop,' that is enough, thank you Dominic,' she said smiling at this small nervous child.

CHAPTER 3
ROLAND AND SAMMY HAVE A RACE TOGETHER

Sammy and Roland's are in class five, they are ready to go home, they also heard the school bell going off, knowing this means they can now all go home now, their teacher Miss Brown has also heard it and announces to the children of Class five. 'You have all heard the school bell ring, so please leave the classroom quietly, and go to the cloakroom, and get your thing's, no need to run in the corridor, I will see you next week, and I hope you all have a good weekend, and come back fully refreshed for a new week,' announces Miss Brown quietly and firmly.

'Yes, Miss Brown, some of them said, the children push their chairs away, from their tables, then each child stands up, to their feet, and one by one left the classroom, and headed to the cloakroom, to pick up their coats.

'Come on Roland, we want to get out, before the rest, of the school come out.' Shouts Sammy, while putting away his books, into his desk.

Roland and Sammy, then head outside, it is Autumn, and they have still, not felt the cold weather yet and did not have the need for a coat. In fact, Roland did have a coat, but he did not want to the cloakroom, to be called names, and he left it behind like Sammy, who was on his heels, going outside, hoping to run, as he still had plenty of energy.

Sammy, has an athletic built, he also has a cheeky smile, Roland is plump, slow with a serious expression on, he has sister Molly who is eighteen months older than him, Sammy's sister Sally is the same age as Molly, they both are in class six.

They all live in a quiet village, which has a beautiful church, The Watermill pub, set near a working watermill, and one small corner shop, a post office.

Eventually, the rest of the school, emerged from the school, Sally, age ten, going on eleven,

she is just like her brother kind, happy with a sweet smile, arrives outside holding hands, with another boy from year seven, Bobby, they stand outside the school, talking to each other.

Molly, also, ten years old, she is not like her brother, but carefree and chatty, arrives out of the school, with five of her friends, one of her friends Olivia, had brought in a batch of homemade biscuits, made by Olivia's Mother, which she shared out with Molly, and her friends.

It is now three thirty -five on a Friday afternoon, the other children are chatting in the playground, with their friends, and some were talking with younger children, who are possibly their younger siblings, waiting for their parents to appear by the gates, a few were running to the gates, where some of the parents were waiting for them, excited that the last hour has gone, and they can all go home.

'I will race you to the gates, 'shouts Sammy, to Roland.

'You know, I cannot run fast', moaned Roland, sadly.

'Yes, you can, just try,' laughed Sammy.

Sammy races ahead, his nimble feet run very quickly, getting closer to the gates.

Roland, tried to keep up with Sammy, he runs as quick as he can, but he only manages to walk slowly, waddling from side to side. Sammy is now getting closer, to the school gates, some of the other parents, are at the entrance of the school gates, watching out, for who was coming out first, most of them were glad to be going home, and getting away from school and the problems, of being there.

Roland's mother was waiting, outside of the gates, watching her son coming towards her, She was standing alongside Laura, Sammy and Sally's mother.

'Got there,' shouted Sammy, touching the school gate post.

Eventually Roland came puffing up, and bent over exhausted, standing close to his mother.

'I told you, I could not run,' groaned Roland, with sweat pouring off his head.

'You may be better, if you did not have those extra chips, at lunch time,' grumbled Sammy.

'I was hungry,' moaned Roland, who was puffing, with exhaustion.

'So was I, I had the first course, and a pudding, and I did not ask for seconds, that is what I had, and you should have had the same, Roland, you are just plain greedy.' Grumbled Sammy, rudely to Roland.

Roland looked sad, he was feeling exhausted, he stood, by his mother hoping, she would notice him, and get some sympathy, from his exhausting run, and maybe Mum, might, have a treat, especially now for doing, this gruelling race, he never felt more, dry and thirstier than he normally did.

he looked up at his Mum, who had now turned away from Roland, talking to Linda, another Mother from School.

Luckily, Kathy did not hear Sammy, say that Roland was greedy, and would have certainly told Sammy off, for being so rude, or did not notice that Roland, was puffed out, from his quick walk, and that he was bending, over getting his breath back.

Kathy was discussing, to Linda, about this new teacher, Miss Mansell.

'I agree, she is not as good as Miss Shepherd, but Miss Mansell, is stricter than Miss Shepherd was ever,' explained Kathy.

Adding, 'Did you know, ' Miss Mansell, said, that Roland, must try better at Science, he loves Science, I think she has a problem with Roland, I have no idea why, Miss Mansell also said, that some children had been saying, that Roland was fat, I do not think that is right, he has a healthy appetite, we do know that, but he was a bonnie baby, which is a good sign, I think she is hearing it's wrong, Roland has never complained about children calling him anything, she must have the wrong child, maybe it was Graham, they we're talking about, groaned Kathy.

'He maybe a little bonnier than Mikki, Lilly's cousin,' lied Linda to Kathy,

'I do not know Lily's cousin,' said a puzzled Kathy.

Mikki is older than Roland, so, I really should not compare an older boy, to your Roland,' said Linda, covering her words up afterwards.

'No, I have never seen your Mikki, then I cannot agree,' Kathy said, replying to Linda.

'Miss Mansell, gave my Tommy four stars, for his exam in Science.' bragged Linda.

Linda said, no more about Mikki, or his weight again.

Kathy was glad to stop talking about Roland, and his body. Roland only had one star, in science, so she said no more about fat or Miss Mansell.

'That is not good,' said Linda, smiling, not realised that Kathy was upset with the fact, her.

Roland was fat, she was thinking perhaps he was fat, looking at him, beside her with his chubby fat legs.

'No, I am not happy at all,' moaned Kathy, I am hoping to see the Head mistress, next week to complain about Miss Mansell, not liking my Roland, and lying about the children calling him names, in a quick breath, she said

Adding, I must go,' said an impatient Kathy.

'Oh! I nearly forgot my Molly, where is she Roland? He was still puffing from his race with Sammy.

'Over there, 'moaned Roland, half looking while being bent over, and pointing to Molly, who was still with her friends munching biscuits.

Roland looking across with envy, at Molly eating a biscuit.

'Can we have those biscuits, when we get home?' grumbled Roland, to Kathy.

'No sorry, Roland they look homemade, we will

make some biscuits on Sunday, when the Silverwood's come to tea, you can have a sandwich, when we get home, and later, we will have a takeaway, when your Dad comes home,' reassured Kathy.

When Wayne comes home from work, he passes Freddie's fry-up café, they do a good take away, then he can treat his family, to a special take away, which he brings home, on the bus, much to annoyance, of some of the passengers, who were aware, of a strong smell of burgers and chips, possibly some of the passengers, might have been vegetarians, and possible find the smell of meat, somewhat sickly.

Laura was watching Roland, and her family, she did not say a word, just astonished, to hear Roland greedy plea, and wanting his sister's biscuit, this child needs to stop having extras, when will Kathy, put Roland on a diet, he is far too fat to even walk, let alone run, even Molly is getting bigger now. I am sorry we must go to tea there on Sundays, I am sure I will say something one day, and upset Kathy, and her family, I am wondering, whatever will they?

be doing next, thought Laura.

Molly comes over, to Roland and Kathy, still munching her biscuit.

'Mm that was lovely, sweet and crumbly', said Molly admitted, smiling to Kathy.

Mum, those biscuits that Olivia's Mum, makes are very yummy, sultanas and icing on top,'

Admits, Molly licking her lips.

Roland looked at Molly, annoyed with her having a biscuit, when he just been running, and needed something sweet, and he was now very thirsty as well.

Earlier his Mum, was talking to her friends, and ignoring him. Roland felt very grumpy, and angry, he was looking down at the ground, thinking what I can do to upset Molly. He has a plan of revenge.

'Come on Children into the car,' urged Kathy, rushing them, both to get into the car, Roland gets in the front with Kathy, and Molly jumps in the back of the car, clutching her favourite toy, Hattie, her toy Koala bear.

'Now Children home, we will go,' shouts Kathy to the children.

'Yes,' they all shout together.

'Now, Children we are having a takeaway, from Freddie's fry-up café tonight, beef burgers, chips and a milk shakes for afters' informs Kathy, remember this was their Friday night treat.

'Hurrah,' shouts Roland.

'Don't forget me,' shouts Molly.

'Of course, you are included silly,' calls back Kathy.

They eventually reach home, and they all get out of the car, and walk towards the house, Kathy puts the key in the door, and push's it open. They all go in, Kathy, heads upstairs to the bathroom, and Molly goes into the lounge, to watch television, she knows that she must wait for Mum, Roland kept back waiting, to go in the kitchen to get some biscuits, which he knew he has some in his own biscuit tin, which used to be full of sweets, and now a biscuit tin, with Roland's biscuits in, the tin has a pattern of toffees, on the front of it.

Molly, knows that soon her meal will be coming, and if she wanted, to have an appetite, for It, she would wait for a big burger and chips, she knew the meal will be arriving , as soon as Wayne get off the bus, at quarter to five. Wayne always finishes early at work, as he starts, At eight quite earlier on Friday.

He is soon due in with the meal, from Freddie's Fryer Cafe any minute now.

Roland is still annoyed with Molly, and wants that biscuit, the one that Molly, had in the Playground.

When everyone is out of his way, and knows that the coast is clear, he rushes over to the Kitchen, and looked in the cupboard, where both their biscuit tins are kept, he finds Molly's tin, tucked behind his, at the back, he moves his tin to one side, and takes out Molly's tin, and plonks it on the table, and then opens it, he spots seven biscuits inside.

'Ah! ha, good,' he cries with glee.

Mollys has a different variety of biscuits, to Roland, he likes the ginger biscuits, and Molly likes the coconut ones, but this time he is determined, to eat at Molly's biscuits, even though these are not his favourite, she can now go without just, like he did today with those home-made biscuits, from a friends mother's house.

Unfortunately, he did not get any biscuits from Kathy, despite his exhausting run, he carefully picks out four of the biscuits from Molly's tin, and quickly gets out his tin, he opens his tin, while balancing it on his lap, he places two of Molly's biscuits into his tin. He then puts his tin back, and goes over to Molly's tin shuts it, and puts it back, where he found it, he stuffs one biscuit in his mouth, while holding the remaining biscuits, in his hand, he puts them in his pocket, and heads upstairs to his bedroom.

He does not feel at all guilty, he knew she has several biscuits, in the playground, and would not find out about the biscuits today. Hopefully, when she did, she would ask Kathy for more.

He sat on his bed, and gobbled them quickly, before Kathy, spotted him, hiding in his bedroom.

But little did Roland know, he had dropped, some of the biscuit inside the bed, on his sheet.

When he got into his bed that night, his mother spotted a bit of biscuit, inside the bed sheet, but said nothing.

In the night, Roland rolled over onto the biscuit, which broke up, over the sheet, inside the bed, he felt the broken biscuit, which was very uncomfortable, he just lay there feeling, very depressed, he hoped his mother would say nothing, if she saw it in the morning, when she makes the bed after he gets up.

He falls asleep very quickly, before brushing away the crumbs, in the night he is restless, and rolling about in his sleep, that night, he woke up in the night, sweating, and sat up, upset with a nightmare, he was having a bad dream about a large biscuit, that ran after him, shouting you have taken my baby biscuits and eaten it.

In the morning Roland got up, as usual to have his breakfast, he was worried, now that Molly would find out, about what he did, and hoped she would forget, how many biscuits, that were in the tin and think she must to eaten them recently.

Molly never found out that morning, but Roland was still thinking about, his biscuit nightmare, this made him anxious, to go into the kitchen, in case he saw this biscuit, from his biscuit nightmare.

That day, life was okay, but being Saturday, sometimes they are going over to Bill's house, and Wayne would be going out with Bill, to do their business, which he told his wife Kathy, but secretly they go down to the pub, and discuss sport, and they smoke, and drink beer, not gone for a business meeting at all.

Roland and Molly, had to play with his daughter and son, while he goes on his 'business trip'.

Roland was still angry with Molly, that he did not want, to sit in the same, car as her, so he had another plan, this plan was that he wanted to hide, and they would think, that Roland, had gone on the bus with Kathy, so when the time came for Wayne and Molly to leave. Kathy had also gone out.

Roland knew where they usually hid, when they played hide and seek, he hoped that no one would go to the airing cupboard, except Kathy when she needed clean linen, he knew that Molly was already in the car, and Wayne was in the house, getting ready for his business talk!!

Roland crept over to the airing cupboard, and climbed up to the first shelf, and hid himself at the back, it was warm and cosy, with blanket and sheets to snuggle into, in fact nice enough to sleep there, all night.

When Wayne was ready to go out, he always shouted, to the children in the lounge, which he did, as normal.

'Come on Children, we are going out,' he shouted up the stairs, and in the lounge.

'Coming Dad, 'shouted Molly back.

Molly walks over to the hallway, and stood, by the door, waiting for Wayne, he came waiting For him.

He has a shave, and a quick wash, and looked very smart, in his clean clothes, and looking tidy and ready to go out.

'Where is Roland? inquired Wayne, looking around for him.

Wayne was very annoyed, all he wanted to do, was to go out soon, he was grumpy, and a very impatient man.

'I have no idea,' replied Molly, worried about where Roland was.

'Go and find him, and tell him to hurry up, we have no time, I am late,' grumbled Wayne, angrily.

Molly runs upstairs and shouted to Roland.

'Roland, Roland, hurry up Dad, is waiting, he is very angry, he wants us now, hurry up.

Molly stood quietly at the top of the stairs, waiting for an answer, or Roland to appear, Still no answers.

Roland, had heard Molly, walking up and down the corridor, but he lay quietly, in the airing cupboard, he felt a sneeze coming on, but he manages to stop it.

Molly was very close, Roland heard her near him, she ran back downstairs, and she got back to Wayne, panting.

'No Sign of him Dad' said Molly, puffing and blowing.

'Oh well, we must go, without him, maybe he went out with Kathy,' grumbled Wayne. very annoyed about Roland making him late for his business meeting.

When they had gone out, Roland heard no noise, and his sneeze returned, antizoo, he sneezed, he nearly fell onto the floor with his giant sneeze, he carefully got down from the cupboard, and crept down stairs, he walked slowly about, looking and listening to make sure they had gone out, in case Molly and Wayne were still about, he was too afraid to go into the kitchen, because of his bad nightmare. he went into the lounge and sat down to watch the television.

Eventually Kathy came back, and went into the lounge, to sit down after her walk back from the bus.

'Roland, what are you doing, back here alone, where is Molly and Dad?' Wailed Kathy

'I do not know,' admitted Roland lying.

'They must have gone to Bill's house without you. I will tell him off when they come home.

Roland sat there getting redder and redder, and worried to what Wayne might do to him, if.

Wayne gets cross, he shouts, and his face looks threating and frightening.

He was to upset to admit, why he was there, but he was still annoyed with Molly.

'I am going upstairs to have my afternoon nap. I will get your food when I come down, 'informs Kathy.

Poor Roland, he was hungry, and thirsty, and could not tell his mum, why he did not get himself anything to eat. Since breakfast., he was feeling horrible after eating, those biscuit's yesterday, the biscuits were not his favourite, and he was tired, and very thirsty, he went upstairs to the bathroom, and turned on the tap, and cupped some water, with his hands, then drinking it.

It was not, what Roland liked, at after all it was water, it had no sweetness to it, but at least he was feeling, less thirsty than before.

He went quietly downstairs, and sat on the sofa, and put on the television, feeling very sorry for himself.

Molly eventually came back with Wayne, and saw Roland on the sofa, watching television.

'Where were you, I looked all over the house for you, but you were not there, did you go out with Mum? shouted Molly.

'No', answered Roland truthfully.

'Then were you then, I had no one to talk to, the two children went outside, to play football, and I was left alone, their Mother took the television upstairs, and watched it in her bedroom,

I had nothing to watch, and nothing to eat., I am starving, I will get some biscuits, from my tin,' grumbled Molly, she stormed out into the kitchen, and opened the cupboard door.

Roland listened quietly, to hear Molly, opening the cupboard, and then to her tin, putting it on the table.

He was thinking, will she ever find out about her biscuits.

Molly came storming back into the lounge, and stood with her arms on her hips, looking angrily at Roland, who just looked at Molly, trying to look completely innocent, she started to shout at Roland.

'All my biscuits have gone, I looked in your tin, and you have two of my coconut biscuits, which are now in your tin. Why did you pinch my biscuit's, you do not like coconut biscuits,'?

shouted Molly, looking at Roland angrily. I am going to tell Mum, when she comes down, grumbled Molly, sitting on the sofa with her arms folded.

Kathy came down two hours later, and Molly got up, and walked over to Kathy.

'Roland has taken my biscuit's and put them in his tin. I have no more biscuits to eat, I did not get any food at the Norman and Betty's house. I did not take my biscuits back, from his tin, because I know that, even that they are coconut biscuits, which are in Roland's tin I cannot steal from him. Mum, can you give me some more biscuits, and hopefully Roland, will not have any of mine again,' pleaded Molly sadly.

'Yes of course darling, I bought some chocolate biscuits, from the shops, with a crisp topping on top, in fact a caramel topping,' reassured Kathy, smiling at Molly.

Kathy and Molly, left Roland on his own, and went to the kitchen to get the biscuits.

When they were in the Kitchen, Kathy gave Molly ten biscuits.

'We will find you a new place for your tin, so you will not have Roland taking them again,' she whispered to Molly.

Roland was in the lounge, now feeling sad, at missing out, on the new biscuits, that Molly had, and he did not.

Molly placed five biscuits, on a plate, and went them into the lounge, and sat with the plate perched on her lap, and ate them in front of Roland, with a large glass of lemonade, beside her on the table, making sure that Roland, saw her biscuits, her lemonade, and her smirk on her face, eating them.

Roland was watching Molly, as she come into the room, he looked at the biscuits, and was very jealous of her, and a drink, which looks like a lemonade, with a straw, a real luxury.

He was feeling horrible, hungry, and fed-up. Life was so unfair; first Molly had a biscuit, from her school mates, and they were nice to her. His friends were rude and not generous, and did not share any sweets with him, and now he was found out, for taking her biscuits.

When will my turn come? grumbled Roland to himself.

Kathy came in, and went over to the chair, where Roland was sitting, he was now looking out of the window, he did not want to see Kathy also having a biscuit, he felt sad and forlorn.

'Roland', said Kathy.

He looked up at Kathy, who was staring down at him, she was annoyed with Roland, for stealing his sister's biscuits. I have given Molly back the biscuits, that you stole from her tin, and as a punishment, you will not have any biscuits, for a week Roland, in fact someone said the other day, that you are far too fat, now I understand what she meant, so having no biscuits for a week, might be a good idea' announced Kathy. looking disappointed at Roland.

Roland said nothing, he just watched Molly, having more biscuits, and wished he had not taken her biscuits, again he was denied of trying out the new biscuits, that Mum has bought, he loved chocolate, and watching Molly have chocolate, left on her face, made him realise how lovely, and chocolaty they were.

Wayne came into the Lounge, he also had the chocolate biscuits, an iced bun and a cup of tea.

Another one of Roland's favourite buns.

Wayne noticed Roland not eating, which surprised him, he knew that Roland was like him, always eating something.

Kathy went back into the kitchen, and brought back a bun, and a cup of tea, for herself and sat down next to Wayne.

Roland, was very upset at seeing his family eating, all his favourite food, his tummy was rumbling, and he knew he had a long wait, for the next meal, this was too much for Roland, he got up and slouched, out of the room, dragging his feet, he went upstairs to his room and sat on the bed and cried .boo hood!!

CHAPTER 4
THE SILVERTON CHILDREN ARE GOING HOME FROM SCHOOL

Following the biscuit situation with Roland, Sammy was waiting at the school gates, with Laura, who is Sammy and Sally's Mother, they were watching, the School children, and looking out for their child to appear, so their parents would pick them up.

Sally, Sammy's sister, is talking to a boy, who is about the same age, as Sally.

Sammy turns to Laura, with a sad face.

'Mum! do we have to go to tea, with the Broome's on Sunday, I hate going to Kathy's house,

It is so hot and stuffy, and her food is so tasteless, Roland is okay to play with, but he all he wants to do is sit on the sofa, and play boring board games, but apart from that, why do we have to go there? moaned Sammy, sadly.

'Sammy, don't worry darling, one day they can come, to our house, and you can show Roland what we get up to, I expect they did not know your Dad, has an indoor golf game, or a table tennis table, set up in the garage, on the other hand, we could make an excuse, and never go to them again, which is a pity, as Sally gets on with Molly, and Kathy has a good heart, and

Wayne is a quiet man, although your Dad has nothing in common, with him, but he does like Kathy, Roland, and Molly.

'You could show him some games, that you play with, and give him some ideas, for an exercise regime, or even take him, for a walk with Brunch,' suggested Laura.

'Yes, good idea, Brunch loves going for walks, I hope he likes Dogs' said Sammy.

'Why did we give our dog, Brunch to Mrs White? asked Sammy, looking at Laura, with a puzzled face.

'We gave him to Mrs White, when she was left, without her husband Adrian, when he sadly passed away. We did not have the time and energy, to take Brunch for walks, being a lively spaniel, who needed to go out for long walks, we could still see him, as much as we like, but not living with us, your Dad, thought that Mrs White, would enjoy him more, than us,' explained Laura.

'But she may let me, take him for a walk, with Roland maybe,' admitted Sammy hopefully.

Sammy, was feeling more positive, about seeing less of Roland, in the future, he was starting to smile, and thinking that he would, have more time to see his other friends, over the holidays.

'Where is Sally? Asked Laura, who was glancing around, the playground, finding it difficult to spot with Sally's uniform, as everyone's looked the same, in theirs, as the other children, in her blue and grey school uniform, I cannot see her, she is camouflage with the other children, I think she has a new boyfriend,' admitted Laura.

'Yes! look, there she is talking, with one of my boyfriends,' said Sammy, pointing to were.

Sally was standing, with a boy from a class above Sally's it is Bobby the boy flirt, I do not know what's she sees in him, Mum,' sighed Sammy, with disgust of his sister, having a boyfriend!!

Laura peered across the playground, and she saw that Sally, who was holding Bobby's hand.

'Well, Sammy, he looks quite sweet,' smiled Laura, admiring Sally's boyfriend, from what she could make out, from his tidy appearance. (Sammy had come out of school, with his shirt

hanging out, and his tie tied, around his waist)

'Hmm, he is clever his brother Adam who is in our class,' said that he is very clever, and a flirt, but do not tell Sally, they call him the flirty Bertie, apart from that, he is just an ordinary boy,' said Sammy, giving a smirk.

'Oh, hurry up Sally, we are waiting for you,' shouts Laura.

'Coming Mum,' called back Sally.

Sally. came running up, Mum I think I am in love,' admits Sally, smiling.

Sammy looked at Sally with contempt.

'Of, course you are darling,' smiles Laura, agreeing with Sally, remembering, that at her age she was the same, and her mother, probably thought that Laura, will soon grow out of this silly behaviour.

'Mum, I just need to ask Bobby something before we go,' said Sally, in a rush.

'Alright, but be quick,' said Laura, quickly.

Sally puts down her school bag and dashed back to

Bobby, who was watching other girls, in the playground.

Sally runs back to Bobby, and tells him about her date, with him next week, he nods his head with agreement.

Sally gives him a kiss on the cheek, and runs back to Laura, and Sammy.

Sammy looks with disgust with Sally kissing Bobby on the cheek.

Bobby slings his bag, over his shoulder, and waves to Sally as he passes the school gates.

Sally, waves back smiling at having a lovely boyfriend.

Bobby heads away from the gates and proceeds down the road.

'Where does Bobby live Sally? Laura asked, curiously, as she watches, Bobby walks quickly down the road.

'He lives over there, with his Mum and Dad, and his baby sister Beth, age two and three quarters, 'informs Sally, pointing to a house, on the corner.

'Very impressive, maybe he can come to tea one day, and we can meet him properly', inquires Laura.

'No, Mum please don't, he would be so embarrassed, and so would I,' said Sally, sadly.

She picked up her bag, and carried it, ready to get back to the car.

'Okay, sorry, just an idea, now we must get back, our car is parked, around the corner, in

Primrose Close, and I need to get back, and put the stew in the oven, otherwise we will have a late dinner,' groaned Laura.

'What do you see in that boy Cass? asked Sammy grumpily.

'I love him,' said Sally, getting upset by Sammy's angry comment.

'Hmmm, what is with girls and love, I am happy kicking a football, I have no interest in girls whatsoever,' brags Sammy.

'Your time will come Sammy, one day you will be besotted with girls, as Bobby is.

Come on you too, let's get home, and get a cup of tea for me, and maybe a piece of me.

Gingerbread cake,' said Laura, picking up Sammy's bag from the pavement.

'I can carry that Mum,' snapped Sammy, taking the bag off Laura.

'I was trying to hurry, you two up,' admitted Laura, quickly, who is getting fed up, with her two awkward children.

'The other day, I was just thinking what well-mannered children I have, maybe I should take back those words, and think of all the other good, things about you.' admits Laura, saying out loud.

'What are we good at? inquired Sally curiously.

'You are good at tidying your rooms, helping with the washing up, sometimes… and helping little old ladies, across the road, knowing that this is a good saying, even when people just say that sometimes.' said Laura.

'When do we do that,' asked Sammy, puzzled at Mum suggestions.

'I am sure you will one day,' laughs Laura.

They proceeded to Primrose Close, which is a good

walk away, from the school.

Sammy walked slowly, behind Sally and Laura.

Laura turns around to Sammy and asks him.

'How much homework, have you got tonight? enquired Laura, to Sammy.

'I have English and Geography, Mrs Morris wants everyone in my class, to draw a map of their birth country? Some of my friends do not come, from this country, so we will all have different pictures, which I am looking, forward to seeing, because we have one child in our who comes from Italy, and they have a country shaped like a boot, and that will be so funny, and one of my friends aunties, comes from New Zealand, and apparently, they have a north island, and a South Island, the north island is hotter, than the South Island, which I call a back to front country,' says Sammy laughing.

'Oh, that is interesting,' said Laura.

'Yes, we have a child from Australia, and Spain also,' admitted Sammy.

'That is good, lots of different countries, I am not to Australia, or New Zealand, but I have been to Spain. It is very hot there, Australia, would be too hot for me, but your Dad.

loves the sun, I prefer Norway, cold and normal, what about you Sally? What homework have you been set tonight? asked Laura.

Sally puts on a sad face, we have got Maths, and some words to learn, for our spelling test, they are very hard Mum!' sighed Sally, making a grimace face.

'Never mind Sally, when you have learnt them, I will test you later,' said Laura sympathetically.

'Thanks. Mum,' said Sally grinning and relieved.

'What is your hardest work, you have been given Sally? asked Laura,

'It is influenza,' said Sally sighing.

That could be difficult, is it a Z, or a S,' enquired Laura.

'Exactly Mum,' admits Sally, walking, and kicking a few leaves, on the pavement.

Miss Harris, said three of the words, may be difficult to learn, horizon, luncheon, and Influenzas,' said Sally, feeling stressed, having to learn all these spelling words.

'I can see, why they are difficult,' agrees Laura.

'That is easy, 'Horizon is H O R E S A N, see Sally no problem,' bragged Sammy, grinning.

'Wrong,' said Laura, looking crossly at Sammy, who pushed Sally as if to say, you are very stupid Sally.

'Oh! Said Sammy, now embarrassed about boasting.

'Well, that is what I would write,' said embarrassed Sammy, feeling silly now he was wrong, and unhappy, that he was not, as clever as he thought.

'No, sorry Sammy, you are only nine years old, you have a lot to learn,' admits Laura, looking angrily at Sammy, for thinking he was right.

'Hmm,' said Sammy, upset by his Mum's remarks…

'Sammy, Horizon is spelt H O R I Z O N, said Laura, pointed out why he was wrong.

'Oh,' said Sammy, feeling stupid, and embarrassed again.

'Mum, that is not all, I must write words, that sound the same, but they have a different meaning,' admits Sally.

'What do you mean,' asked Laura, quite puzzled by Sally's homework.

'I must find another word, which sounds like Key, (the one that you need to open a door,)
But a word that is relates to the sea, I think, so I which I think Mum it is Q U A Y,' said.
Sally spelling out the word.

'That one was easy, this word that sounds like a CELL, (a small room fit for a monk.) what is another word, used in a shop, that sounds like CELL, is it S E L?' Said Sally spelling that word.

'Right! Said Laura, you know lots of Sally, we could find words that Miss Morris, does not give you, and show her that you, have learnt more, than she gave you, to prove that you have done more for your homework, than your friends in the class, and maybe you may get an A for your efforts?'

'I now know what you mean, we can find other words for you, but I will not give you the spelling the same, let me think which words, mean a different meaning, but sounds the same maybe Sammy, can do this one, maybe it is harder than you think. Sammy spells another word for rain, (meaning the weather,) the equivalent on a horse's item.' Asked Laura.

'Oh, that is difficult,' said Sammy, biting his lip, with concentration.

'I know it,' it is R E I N,' Sally said, spelling it out loud.

'Wait I nearly got it,' shouts Sammy, looking angry with Sally again.

'I have already done it, silly, you were not listening,

about my word, 'grumbled Sally.

'Oh, you are too quick,' said Sammy grumbling, he was upset that Sally, got the spelling first.

'Well done! Sally, I will give you a good mark, if you were in my class,' smiles Laura.

'Thanks Mum,' said Sally, giving her mum a big hug.

Sammy looked on, feeling very disgruntled.

They arrive at the car,

'Can I sit in the front Mum,' begs Sally, Sammy sat in it this morning, it is my turn, Mum moans Sally.

'Okay,' replies Laura, she opens the door, with the car keys, and gets in.

Sally gets in the car, and sits next to Laura, in the passenger seat, who is in the driving side.

Sammy reluctantly sits at the back, and sits staring at Sally, very angry, because he has been shown up as stupid by Sally…

'I can see the back of your head,' shouts Sammy, and you do not know, what I am doing.

Shouts Sammy.

Sally turns around, to see what Sammy is doing.

'Why are you sticking out, your tongue out at me, Sammy,' asked Sally curiously.

'Because you made me so angry,' shouts Sammy, loudly.

'Oh, shut up Sammy, you are annoying me,' moans Sally.

'Now, stop it you two, we will be home soon, and I want you both to be kind, and stop.

All your quarrelling, when we go over to the Broome, family on Sunday, and I want you to show them how to behave properly,' prompted Laura.

The two children, sat quietly throughout the journey, Sally looking out of the side window, and Sammy was looking out, of the other window.

As they passed the fields, Sally shouts 'I can see the Twinkle the horse first,' shouts Sally.

'Hmm, I must have missed it', moaned Sammy, sighing.

'I saw it first,' shouts Sally bragging.

' Now, now children, we must stop having competitions, about Twinkle the horse, yes, I know that means, we are nearly home, shall we find something else, to represent going home, how about instead of horses, you sit back, and shut your eyes, and wait for the car to turn the corner, you will know, when I turn the corner you will sway, to the left slightly, and then you can open your eyes, and that will mean we are home,' no more who sees what, just be quiet, and shut your eyes, until we get home,' suggests Laura.

Sally, turns around, and stuck out her tongue at Sammy, who was looking sad, and unhappy.

Laura spotted Sally, sticking out her tongue at Sammy.

'Now, now, no more sticking out tongues, you two,' said Laura, getting bored with the two quarrelsome children.

'I will if you will, Sammy,' moans Sally.

'OK!' shouts Sammy, sitting back on his seat, with his arms folded.

The children shut their eyes, and wait for a gently sway to the left, eventually they feel the sway to the left,

and when they knew, that they are nearly home, they opened their eyes, and they both Shouted home!!! together, then the car drove down the drive, and arrived back to their house.
The Orange Tree House.

CHAPTER 5
THE SILVERWOOD FAMILY GET TOGETHER

The next day after they had come home, and had got back, to being nice to each other again.

Laura is in her kitchen making breakfast for Sammy and Sally.

Husband Steve comes in the kitchen, and helps himself, and makes himself a coffee drink, from a kettle nearby, he takes his drink, back to the table, where Sammy and Sally, are sitting.

Steve ruffling Sammy's hair, as he sits down near Sammy.

Sammy, looks up, and grins at Steve.

'Hi Dad, replies to Sammy.

'Hello son,' Steve, sits down to the table, Sally is telling everyone, that she is on a diet, and she only wants, toast and a smear of jam.

Laura comes over to Steve, after putting on the kettle, she hands down a bowl of cereal to

Sammy, who smiles back with gratitude.

'Steve darling what do you want for your breakfast? Asked Laura.

Laura, then runs through the choices, she has to offer, orange juice, cereal or a fried breakfast, Sally is happy just to eat toast with low fat margarine, and some marmalade, Sally thinks she is too fat.

Steve looks up at Laura, and says, 'I will have a fried breakfast, my stomach was rumbling yesterday at work, one of my colleagues, teased me about my rumbling tum, and mentioned to me, saying, 'isn't your missus, giving you enough to eat these days Steveo,' said Steve.

Sally looks up, and asks Steve 'why does he call you Steveo? Dad?

'His accent Sally,' replies Steve.

'What is an accent' asked Sally, looking puzzled.

'He has a Welsh accent, it is the way they pronounce, the sound of certain words.,' he replies.

'Oh, we have a Welsh girl at school, we laugh at her sometimes, when she speaks funny,'

Said Sally, munching her toast.

'You should not laugh at her, she comes from a family, that speaks like that, if you come from France to a school out there, you may be teased about your accent there' says Steve sternly.

'Oh,' said Sally now feeling bad about, Selwyn, the Welsh girl from school.

Sammy was listening hard.

'Dad, what accent, do we have then,' he asked, cocking his head to one side.

Steve, looked at Sammy, 'I do not know, just normal,'

'Well, Roland speaks with a strange voice, Sammy replies, he was thinking doesn't, everyone has an accent.

'Not strange, just different, Roland has his own accent, Sammy,' replies. Steve correcting Sammy.

'I will ask him,' announced Sammy, curiously.

'I would not do that, that is not a good idea, Sammy,' replies Steve.

'Why not! asked Sammy, looking puzzled.

'He may not like him, asking that, his parents may be offended,' admitted Steve, hoping this accent subject must stop, before anyone else is offended, with this question.

Sammy decided not to ask, any more questions about accents.

Laura, came over with Steve's breakfast,

'Excuse me, I must get for school,' said Sally, getting ready up from the table,

'Thank you darling, could you remind me Laura, to cut the lawn tomorrow, the lawn looks small now the grass has grown, and the weeds have taken over, I need to do some weeding, on the vegetable garden, and the swing needs a new rope, that reminds me, the hedge needs cutting, now that the birding season is over.

'Yes, some one up our road, cut the hedge to soon, and I found a baby bird, on the pavement,

I told the owner of the house, but she did not think, that it was her fault, just an unfortunate accident, silly women,' moaned Laura.

'Was the bird alright?' asked Sammy anxiously.

'I have no idea, I did not see her again,' answered Laura.

'How big is our garden? asked Sammy, changing the subject.

'A quarter of an acre,' replies Steve stretching out his arms, knowing this is not true, but another way of saying very big.

'Miss Brown wants us to do some measuring, for our homework, we are doing some work, on numbers, size of houses, types of houses, and buildings,' said Sammy.

'Well! tell Miss Brown our house is detached, and we have a quarter of an acre of land, at the back, and a small garden at the front., Sammy,' said Laura.

'Right, that sounds big, some of the children in our class, only live in a flat, and they have no garden,' admitted Sally.

'We are lucky then, we have a swing, and trees, but we cannot climb them, as they are only small fruit trees,' announces Sammy.

'Yes, but your Dad had to work hard, to get this big house, and garden,' admits Laura.

'I have parents that gave me, a good education for me, to get a training, and go to university.

So, Sammy if you work hard, you will be able to afford a nice house, for your family, smiles Steve.

'I AM NOT GETTING MARRIED, I AM GOING TO BE SINGLE, AND HAVE A BIG HOUSE, AND A BIG GARDEN, AND I AM GOING TO LIVE THERE, ALL BY MYSELF, 'shouts Sammy, and then he said, I do not like girls, I will have you, Dad, Mum, and Sally can come over for a holiday, but the rest of the time, I will just be lazy.

'Really, Sammy I am surprised no wife, no children,' said Laura sadly.

'Oh, I may have a big dog for company' added Sammy,

No more was said about this subject.

Today, Steve goes to work on public transport, he

leaves the car at home with Laura, she can then take the children, to school by car, and that gives her a chance, to do her shopping, or go to an afternoon class to keep fit, Laura loved history, and once a week, she reads to adults about local History, at her local library.

Steve has the car when the children are on holiday, by then when Laura classes finish, from her team times. Laura and Steve, shop together at the weekend, bringing the children, and teaching them about the food, they buy, this shows them about how, to buy cheap options, and other shopping tips.

Laura, is happy to stay at home, looking after her family, she manages the house, cooking and keeps the house clean and tidy.

Before she got married Laura was a PA, in a very big office sorting out the staff, and helping her boss, on travel trips to America, this is where she met Steve in a bar, waiting for her boss, to discuss travel plans to France, Steve was just having a drink after work, Laura was alone, and spoke to Steve, at the bar, who was also getting a drink, he noticed Laura, alone, and he casually asked her if he could join her.

Laura is now a contented lady, she loved her children, and always wanted a large family, but she thought that after having two, that they would stop, and thinks if she did, then they may need to move, but her house is so nice, she knows she may not get another house, with all the benefits of being close to the children's school, and Steve been close to the train station.

Laura enjoys doing gardening, and experimenting with cooking different dishes, making on occasional cakes, using fresh fruit, and vegetables, which makes healthy cakes, she has used.

beetroot, carrot, apples, and pineapples, and occasionally parsnips.

Laura likes her house smelling fresh, she keeps it clean sometimes using natural ingredients to clean her house, lemon, salt bicarbonate soda, and vinegar, so her house does not have any bad chemicals on the surfaces, as her Mother used to say, I use good old carbolic soap, it kills all germs, and it makes a good lather for hand washing my clothes.

Steve brings in flowers from the garden, into the house, to add to the fresh aroma of Laura's hard working clean house.

Laura, feels having fresh flowers in the house,' is the icing on the cake,' an expression her lovely mother used to say, when Laura's father used to bring fresh flowers into their house,

Laura's father had a love of carnations, and others summer flowers from his garden, and had an also has a vegetable plot.

Laura, gives her family good wholesome meals, she makes all her meals from scratch, only buying good fresh ingredients, and makes sure she does not waste food, if possible, she gives

her family lots of crunchy snacks, apples, carrots, and celery dips trying out new recipes, with new fruits and vegetables, cooking in different way, so make the whole experience of eating was fun and exciting.

After picking up the children from School, and arriving home, Laura gives her children good wholewheat bread sandwiches with tuna, tomatoes, avocado, pine nuts, sometimes may with mayonnaise dressing, and feta cheese, apples and a banana each, she gives them a drink, she makes as fruit smoothies as she prepared, she looks after her husband well too, making sure he is given the right healthy meals, so he can keep fit and well, for his stressful his job, being a good wife, giving them the right nutrients to fight any diseases, she knows what to give to get them well again. For relaxation, Laura has classical music playing in the background, she hopes, that this music will help the children enjoy classical music, Steve enjoys this music, also, in the evening to relax by

The Silverwood children loved going for long walks with their parents.

They both enjoy taking their children, on interesting walks, pointing out different types of birds, plants, and trees, to the children.

After an exhilarating walk, which gives them a good colour, to their cheeks, this helps them have a hearty appetite, if it is a cold walk, they all usually all tired and hungry, after a long walk, Laura would have prepared in advance, something ready to serve them all, when they get back, some hot homemade soup, with bread, fresh from the baker, with cheese, and a light salad, followed by a hot steam treacle pudding, with warm custard, as their Sunday walk treat.

They are a happy and contented family, thinking that most people had similar lifestyle, as themselves. But there was an exception to this, not everyone followed their way of living.

Their children friends' parents do not follow this example, they have a different way of feeding their families.

CHAPTER 6
ROLAND HAS A BIRTHDAY PARTY

Today is Roland's birthday and Roland has invited a few friends over for a party with games, followed by a big birthday teatime spread, with the normal birthday cake, and candles.

Kathy has tried to cook a cake for Roland, which she did of a fashion, a rather clumsily iced one, it wasn't a professional looking one, just the standard of an average bought variety.

Kathy managed to buy several different colour balloons, and blew up all of them with of colours, of red, pink, yellow, blue and white balloons and tied them outside the house on the hedges, and a streamer across the front doorway, displaying the words.

'**HAPPY BIRTHDAY**' printed in a bright blue colour, on a white background, she did this on the night before his birthday, so it would surprise him on his actual birthday.

The other red and white balloons were inside the house, with another banner inside stating that it is, '**ROLAND'S BIRTHDAY TODAY**' this time written in big bold gold letters, on a pale blue background displayed over the lounge doorway.

Before the children arrived at the house, Kathy had

put on a musical cassette of children's nursery rhymes playing on it, this would be a welcome for the children arriving there.

Roland had asked fifteen children to come to his party, but only ten decided to come, and of course Sammy was the first on Roland birthday list.

The children arrived at Roland's house one by one, either with a Mother, Father, a big brother, or big sister.

Roland and his Mother, stood standing at the door, greeting each child, as they arrived, Roland, showed each child into the sitting room, first taking the presents off them, Roland then throwing the presents down on a vacant sofa, inside the hallway.

Roland was strutting around, telling the children to make sure that they were all, seated on the

floor, ready for the conjuror to perform his magic tricks, this task of the children arriving made,

Roland feels very important, bossing the children, to sit on the floor, and telling them to behave themselves as instructed by Kathy.

As it was a Saturday, Wayne, Roland's father was banned from coming into the sitting room, as he had been drinking earlier that day, and was happy sleeping in his bedroom, away from everyone, where no one heard him, snoring, his snoring was an equivalent to a motor bike, roaring down the road. Wayne was glad to be upstairs away from noisy excitable children, with his headache from drinking, there was no place for him to stay, but quietly upstairs asleep.

Sammy came over with Laura, all dressed in his best suit, blue shirt, and his brand-new red tie, looking very smart, Roland was excited to see Sammy, who was clutching a big lumpy present, he knew his present we're going to be good, as he knew the family, and all the nice toys that Sammy and Sally had in their playroom.

'Hello! Roland, I have got you a very special birthday present, I hope you like it,' he said handing it over to Roland.

Sammy was excited at giving the present as much as Roland was for receiving it.

Roland felt the package, it was very lumpy.

'Ooh how exciting, can I open it now,' he asked Sammy very excited and impatient.

Kathy overheard Sammy and Roland talking about the present.

Kathy knew that Laura would have bought an expensive present for Roland, and was keen to see the present herself later, as Laura being her friend the present would probably be a very expensive one.

'Sorry, Roland, could you put Sammy's present with your other friends presents, they are all the same, you can open it later, you need to be with your friends in the living room,' ordered Kathy.

Roland face dropped, with disappointment, he sulked in front of Sammy, walking past him, feeling very sorry for himself. Sammy knew all about Roland difficult nature, he was upset with Roland for being so silly and childish about his present, Sammy went to join his friends,

in the lounge.

Roland came back to look outside to check if there were any more children to arrive, he left Kathy and walked down the path, looking down the road to see if any more children we're coming, to his house,

'Are there any more children coming to my party Mum?' asked Roland.

'Yes, there is one more expected to come, which is Ronnie' explained Kathy, patiently waiting with Roland who had come back from going down the garden path.

Ronnie was one of Roland's classmates, he was one of the bright children in his classroom, who always had a ready smile, his hair was always a beautiful shiny auburn hair. Ronnie was eventually coming down Roland's path towards the house, which pleased Roland.

Roland was watching as Ronnie and his Mother saunter slowly towards the house, he was.

wondering why he was carrying a bunch of flowers, was that my birthday presents a bunch of flowers thought Roland, Kathy thought the same, but he was anyway very cross at Ronnie for being so late and holding up his conjuror.

Ronnie grinned at Roland, pleased to be asked to his birthday party do.

Ronnie was excited to seeing the banner and all the colourful balloons, all over the garden, it made him get in the mood for a happy time with his friends and see Roland who was one of his second-best friends who like Sammy was a kind child, but always thought Roland could have been treated better by his other classmates.

As he was approaching, with a wide grin on his freckled face, he is wearing a smart well ironed green shirt, and brown trousers, a bright orange bow tie with white spots dotted over it, neatly wound around his neck, proudly carrying a bunch of flowers.

'Hurry up Ronnie, we are waiting to get started, the conjuror is getting angry,' lied Roland looking very cross, jumping up and down, but glad he arrived eventually to getting started with his party, and his much-awaited tea and birthday cake, and see magic tricks which he also wanted to witness.

'Hello Ronnie, you are the last child to arrive, the conjuror is waiting to start,' admitted.

Kathy, knowing that Roland was getting impatient and angry.

'Oh, I am so sorry we are late, but Ronnie insisted on picking you some flowers from our garden,' said a very apologetic Mrs Chadwick, pushing Ronnie quickly forward.

'Here you are Mrs Broome,' said Ronnie grinning with wide toothy grin, thrusting a bunch of flowers into Kathy's hand.

Kathy looked down at the wet bunch of daisies, that had been picked that morning.

'Oh! Thank you, Ronnie, how kind you are,' admitted Kathy, quite overwhelmed with embarrassment at such a kind act from a child.

Kathy was very moved by Ronnie kind gesture, she had never been given flowers by anyone not even Wayne, or her children before.

Mrs Chadwick wished Roland a happy birthday.

Roland wasn't interested in her wishes, just Ronnie who at last had arrived and now they could get on with his party and the conjuring tricks, who he wanted to hurry up and come inside, so the conjuror could start his magic.

Mrs Chadwick told Ronnie a few words before walking briskly away.

'Bye Mum see you at six,' shouted Ronnie, waving at her leaving him.

Mrs Chadwick was glad to get some housework done before picking Ronnie up as he is an active child who needed lots of time and energy with his parents, as he had to be occupied and taken out a lot. Mrs Chadwick could go home and have a well-deserved cup of tea before starting her housework that had been neglected from Ronnie because of all the time in occupying him.

Kathy stood for a minute, left with her flowers, contemplating where was she going to put theses flowers, she smelt them, and wondering about where to put them, she went inside and took them into the house, having never owned a vase to be able to put them in.

Kathy disappeared into the kitchen thinking of putting her daisies into a pot, or container.

She managed to find an old jam jar and popping them in, thus filling it up with water and placing the jam jar on the kitchen windowsill.

Ronnie followed Roland into the living room.

Kathy went back into the lounge, having checked the food, making sure it was ready for the children later.

When all the children had appeared to be all here, Kathy told the children, we will start with a conjuror then tea, after that we will have pass the parcel and musical chairs.

The conjuror had arrived earlier and was sat waiting to see all the children, who were ready for an afternoon of magic. The conjuror was a tall man, and dressed for the part, in a black suit, a black top hat covered with glitter and stars, his suit was dotted with pictures of playing cards all over his top jacket, with a flower in his buttonhole, which was a trick plastic flower, that squirted water if a child went close to it to smell it.

The conjuror was tall man, who played the part of a conjuror, although he was really Dennis the Plumber.

'Hello Children, I am Tizzy Whizzy your conjuror, he said shouting to the children, who sat looking up at the conjuror, from down on the floor.

He looked slightly nervous, not knowing what to expect, from these strange children he never met before.

'Hello' shouted the children, back to Tizzy Whizzy.

He started to remove his conjuring props, from a large box on the floor, the first trick, he pulled out of his box, was a book, he opened it, he then showed the children the book, it revealed black and white pictures, the children, whispered, oohs and hash.

'Now, children, these as you see, are a black and white picture book, he shows the children letting all the children see the black and white book, and the pages inside, he shuts the book then he asks the children, to say abracadabra.

Then, all the children, then shouted " ABRACADABRA," he waves his wand, over the book, he then opens the book, and by magic the pages in the book, changed from black and white pictures to colour one, he shows the children, having explained to the children, it was their clever abracadabra words, that changed the black and white pictures into colour, which made the children laugh, they looked at each other, with amazement, isn't that clever, one child said to another child, who also looked pleased, at their clever words.

Next the conjuror takes off his black hat, then turns it upside down, and placing a scarf over the up turned hat, and he asked the children again, to say abracadabra, they shouted.

ABRACADABRA again, he then pulled out a white dove, from his hat, and

balanced the dove on his hands, moving the hand, sideways, to show the children the dove the dove starts to flap his wings, but Tizzy Whizzy, hold it back, with his hand.

The children shouted, and clapped, with joy.

Dennis the Plumber is doing these tricks for free, but in exchange for his service he said, he would do it, if Kathy, gave him a sandwich, and cup of tea.

Kathy, said if you want you can have some jelly and ice-cream, but the conjuror, said a cup of tea, and a sandwich will be fine, thank you kindly.

Roland, was getting bored, and hungry, with these tricks, he got up, hoping no one would notice him, he crept quietly into the kitchen, he knew that his Mum, had sat down, also watching Tizzy Whizzy, Roland managed to go in the kitchen, with neither Kathy, or the children watching him, go in the kitchen, and spot a plate of biscuits, he put his hand on the plate, and grabbed quickly six biscuits, and slipped them, into his pocket, he also took a handful, of salted peanuts, from a bowl nearby, Roland sneakily came back, to the room, where all his friends were, he stood at the back of the room, against the wall, out of sight of his friends, he managed to slip, some biscuits and peanuts, carefully into his mouth, hoping no one would notice him, he carried on watching his friends, talking together, about the great magic being performed.

Sammy did notice Roland, slip into the kitchen, and watched at Roland tactics, he was disgusted with Roland, for scoffing food, without sharing it with anyone.

Roland saw Sammy eventually looking at him, he had no idea he had upset, his friend Sammy, and wondered why he looked so angry.

When all the tricks had been performed Kathy went over to the Tizzy Whizzy and said, 'Thank you, Tizzy Whizzy, for your magic tricks, that was very good, even I did not know how you did it, would you like your cup of tea, and sandwich now, she asked him to smile.

Kathy was happy at making the children enjoy his magic tricks.

'A pleasure Mrs Broome,' admitted Dennis smiling at Kathy.

When the conjuror had packed up, his things, and drank a cup of tea, and ate his sandwich, And quickly finished his snacks, he left after Kathy, he wasn't keen, to stay any longer on ten children, roaming around, making a noise.

'Say bye, to the conjuror children,' ordered Kathy.

'Bye Mr Tizzy Whizzy.' They said and waved to him.

'Bye chidden, he said shouting back, Mr Tizzy Whizzy and left the house.

Kathy watched Dennis leave the room, when she heard him slam the outside door and left, she knew it was time for tea.

Kathy clap ped her hands and shouted at the top her

voice.

'Now, children we can now all sit down to tea, go through this door, she said, pointing to dining room door.

Adding 'everything is laid out on the table, sandwiches, biscuits, jelly, crisps, and of course, Roland's big birthday cake, with ten candles on it, as Kathy had made it, she hoped it was good enough to eat.

Kathy pushed the dining room door open, the children rushed through, into the dining room, and scrambled, onto the chairs, one boy dashed to sit at the top of the table, where the cake was, which happened to be Roland's seat.

Roland, saw the boy, sitting comfortably on his chair, Charlie was unaware that Roland, was about to get angry and pull him off the chair.

Roland rushed over to his Charlie, and shouted, at him.

'No!! you cannot sit there it is my seat and it is my party, and that is where the cake is. shouted Rolland, at the boy.

Roland, tried to remove Charlie, off the chair, by pulling his cardigan, the boy held on tight but eventually he fell off the chair, on to the floor.

Kathy rushed over, and managed to get the child get off the floor, he stood up, standing he

looks across at Roland, who was standing by, to retrieve his chair, Roland quickly jumped on the chair, before the child returned.

Charlie started to cry, and shout, 'I want my Mummy' he boos hooded, with tears running, down his face, Kathy was not a person to know how to comfort a child, so she is moved.

Charlie swiftly to another chair.

Kathy said to Charlie, 'you sit here, and she put Charlie, a long way away from Roland, who was sat at the top of the table by now, looking very smug, at having his seat returned to him.

Roland, looked down towards, the end of the table, showing that he is was, the king of the

castle, and that no one, must come near his seat again, expression. All children were afraid that Roland would be nasty to them too.

Kathy announced, to the children, who heard her speak, and they looked up at Kathy speaking, but not Roland, as he was angry with her, for being nice to Charlie.

'Now children just tuck in, and in a minute, we will light the candles on Roland's cake.

Kathy was relieved that everyone, had now tucked into the food, and that Charlie, was.

Having something to eat, and looked happier, since Kathy has managed to sneak him, a square of chocolate, that she carefully gave Charlie secretly.

When the children we are nearing the end of the crisps and sandwiches.

Kathy had been watching the children, eyeing the cake and thinking, when are we going, to have it soon, so she decided that it was time to light Roland's cake.

Kathy got out a box of matches, and came over to light the candles, she bent over Roland and carefully lit the candles.

She asked Roland, 'You can blow out the candles, but

try and blow all the candles, in one go and make a wish, but do not tell anyone.

Roland stood up, and bent over the cake, and blew out the candles, he did not manage, it in one go, and blew again, eventually the cake candles were all blown out.

Kathy applauded, well done to Roland, she smiled with admiration to her Roland, no one else in the room clapped, she was on her own clapping,

Kathy then cut the cake, Roland waited for his cake, to come to him first.

Roland looked at Kathy, showing that he wanted a big slice of this cake, so he puts on his sad face to Kathy.

'Can I have a large piece of cake, I am so hungry,' moaned Roland, looking at his mother mournfully.

Kathy had not noticed in the kitchen the bowl of peanuts, that had got lower, in the dish, or the number of biscuits that had gone.

'Of course, darling Roland, and Molly, can have a large piece of cake too, she did not realise, what she was doing, by giving her children, big slices of cake.

Kathy cut two larges' slices, making sure, that Roland had the biggest, of the two slices, and

Another large slice went over to Molly.

Kathy, then cuts the cake equally, for the rest of the children, but because of the large slices.

that went to Roland and Molly, there were hardly any left for the other children, the children only had a sliver piece of the cake each/

Kathy finished handing out to the rest of the children who were watching Kathy divided the cake between them, waiting patiently, for the remainder of the cake to

71

go to them.

Roland stuffed his cake, into his mouth, swallowing it almost, in one mouthful, the rest of the children were upset to see, compared with Roland and Molly, their size of the cake, was so small no bigger than a two large postage stamps.

After tea, the children returned to the sitting room, and waited till Kathy had, more surprises lined up ready for them.

'Now children would you like to all, sit in a circle on the floor and, we will play pass the parcel.

All the children were excited with this game, as they knew that one of them, would get a present.

Kathy reached up to a shelf, and took down a parcel, which was wrapped neatly in brown paper tied up tightly with white string wound around the big package, she it took over to the children, who were sitting watching Kathy come over with it, and they wondered who was going to be handed the package first, they we're looking happy, to play pass the parcel.

They waited patiently for one of them, to have the parcel on their laps.

'Now children, here is the parcel, and she handed it down, to one child, all the children in the circle we're looking at the exciting parcel, which had layers of brown paper, it was large, but disguised to how big, the present was, or what it contained.

Kathy goes to the radio, and switches on some music, she then turned the knob to start the Music playing.

'Now children pass the parcel around, to the child on your left,' announced Kathy, watching carefully to make sure this is properly managed.

Kathy started the music, and then the parcel gets passed around, and after a minute, of passing the parcel around, Kathy was watching the parcel coming towards Molly, she stopped the music, and Molly, was the first to take off the paper with gusto, and threw the paper behind her, then the music restarted again, either landing on Molly's lap or Roland's lap.

After seven papers were screwed up on the floor behind them, the next paper to come off would eventually be the last wrappings, so the music continued with Kathy stopping and starting the music, when it was either Roland or Molly's lap, that she stopped it at.as it was

Roland's birthday, and she knew that Roland would make a fuss it he was not given a present, when it got to Roland's lap, Kathy stopped the music, and Roland undid the parcel.

All children kept hoping that the music, would stop on their lap, but no, it was fell mostly on Roland, or Mollies lap. Eventually with the last wrapping, it stopped at Roland, he quickly opened the wrapping, from the parcel, the parcel contained a bag of chocolates.

'Oh" he opens the box, and held it open, to show the children, some of the children, said.

Oh! He then shouted with joy, 'Oh, goody chocolates all for me,' he squealed with joy, he was very excited, it was a large bag, of mixed chocolates, the flavours were orange, toffee, strawberries, coconut, flavours, the nutty chocolate, they all had a gold wrapping on them.

'OH, lovely all my favourites', shouted Roland, who whooped with joy.

Roland stood up, and got to his feet, and rushed swiftly, as he was able, holding the bag of chocolates with him, he walked quickly, into his bedroom which was upstairs, he threw the bag of chocolates onto his bed, and came downstairs, and returned back to the party, the children who were still sat down, amazed at Roland's quick exit, he sat down puffing, and glad he was had managed to remove, his chocolates, without sharing them, with his friends

at the party, they were safely on his bed, knowing, that no one would see them, or consume them.

Kathy looked on, with amazement at Roland, who had made a quick exit, with the chocolates, she looked at the other children's faces, who had also watched him run upstairs into his bedroom, she was flabbergasted, but said nothing, and without a further ado Kathy, called to the children, and announced to them, now children, hoping to change the subject of

Roland's run into his bedroom, with his chocolates.

Kathy clapped her hands; we will now be playing musical chairs.

'Next, children grab a chair, we need two rows of chairs, back-to-back.

All the children got up, and went to the back of the room, and they each picked up a chair.

Then they arranged the chairs in two long rows.

Roland, no need to get a chair, we want one less,' announced Kathy.

The children stood around waiting for the music to start.

Kathy went to her tape, and put on the music, the

children walked, around the chairs,

expecting the music to stop any minute. Kathy turned off the music, this went on to the last three chairs, with Roland and Lucy, Katie and Mary, were the last four children left, eventually it came to the last two chairs, with Roland, Michael and Lucy, who were the last ones to get the chairs, Lucy sat quickly, and held her chair tight hoping that Roland wasn't going to pull her off this chair, like he did with Charlie.

'Roland off you go,' ordered Kathy.

Roland looked at his mother, with anger at being told to sit down, with a raging face, he sat down on the floor with the rest of the children, with his arm tightly folded.

The last chair was left with two children being left, one child who was first to sit on it, was a child called Lucy, and Michael, who did not manage to sit on it first. He had to sit down with the rest of the children,

This time Kathy, could not control who won, it was a little girl named Lucy she smiled at

Kathy, saying she was glad to sit down, she was a delicate looking child, the noise, and the children, rushing about upset Lucy and she went over to Kathy, waiting for her present who handed down to Lucy a box of coloured pencils, she looked pleased, with her present, and thanked Kathy, quietly.

The rest of the day, the children, just sat and chatted to each other, Roland sneaked back to his bedroom, whilst he was inside, he shut the door, for some privacy, and took a couple of chocolates, from his bag of chocolates, and sat on his bed eating, them, he managed to eat four, before Kathy shouted to Roland, ' where are you Roland, the children are going home now.

Roland came out of his bedroom from being upstairs, he had chocolate smeared all over his mouth, and his teeth smothered in chocolate too.

Sammy, watched Roland, emerge downstairs from his bedroom, with a red face, who was covered in chocolate, which looked very messy.

Kathy looked at Roland face, and she said nothing, she wasn't surprised, with his chocolate face which was, smeared with chocolate, whom, she has seen many times.

The children eventually went home, one by one, with their parents, who thanked Kathy, for having their child to the party.

Sammy was the last child to leave the party, he stood patiently at the door, hoping the next parent to come was Mother, he nearly gave up hope of seeing her come, when he thought he would go in the sitting room and watch the television with Roland, whom at this moment had lost his faith in Roland's being his friend again.

Laura came rushing in,' I am sorry for being late Sammy.

'I hope you had a lovely time,' she said puffing, with all her running.

Roland had gone back upstairs to his bedroom, so, he was nowhere to be seen, he was not waiting for his friend to go, Roland wanted to eat more chocolates.

'Laura asked Kathy 'How are you? She admired the balloons on the hedges outside.

They are so pretty; you must have needed a lot of puff to blow up so many 'Laura inquired.

'Yes, it was difficult with all that blowing up

balloons, I am completely exhausted, I will have a nap this evening, then I will have a big bowl of ice-cream,' admitted Kathy looking tired, with grey rims under her eyes.

'Thank you for having Sammy, he looks tired, so you must have exhausted, his energy,' implied Laura.

'Yes, we did have a lot of games, where the children were running around,' admitted Kathy.

'Sammy will probably have a good sleep, Sammy likes to run about, he has a lot of surplus energy to get rid of,' smiled Laura, hoping that Kathy, may say something similar about her children and hear some good news about Roland's diet plan.

'Oh,' Roland has bags of energy too,' admitted Kathy, lying.

Laura said nothing, *she was thinking, yes Roland, eats so much he will have lots of energy. but does not do a thing about it.*

Sammy, said goodbye to Roland, who was now come back, who stood beside Kathy, hearing.

Laura, talking to Kathy, at the door, he was standing by his mother, looking pleased to see all.

His friends leave, and now it is possible to scoff more chocolates, and sweets.

Sammy, walked back to the car, with Laura, who was now looking at his sad face, seeing that had been to a party with children, and eating nice food, and should be happy, going to see his friends and have a nice tea party.

When they got in the car, Sammy sat next to Laura.

Laura noticed that Sammy was still quiet and sad.

'Sammy, did you enjoy the party,' enquired Laura,

wondering why he had a sad face.

Sammy, said nothing, at first, and then he burst out.

'No! mum I did not, Roland was utterly rude, nasty, and greedy, he had the biggest slice of cake, most of the prizes, and if he did not win a prize, he sulks and made all his friends, upset and sad.

'Really Sammy, and we are going to his house again, next week, I hope you will be coming, despite what you just said,' said Laura sympathetically.

'Mum, please count me out, I do not want to go, with this spoilt child again,' said Sammy.

sadly.

Laura, said nothing again, and when they got home, Sammy went to his room.

The next morning Sammy and Sally went to school as usual. Roland was not at school, which did not surprise Sammy, after he ate lots of cake, chocolates, crisps, and biscuits on his birthday.

The teacher looked up, at the class, as was she was marking off the register, she announced she could not see Roland was here.

Sammy stood up, pleased to make this announcement about Roland, about this greedy child.

'I expect Roland, has a big tummy ache, from the amount of food, he ate on his birthday,

Miss Morris,' he announced, angrily, he still had not forgiven Roland for his behaviour on Saturday.

Later that day, Miss Morris came over to Sammy.

'Sammy you were right about Roland, he did have a tummy ache, he won't be at school for a few days, his Mother told the school, on the phone this morning, Miss

Brackett the secretary.
told me this morning about Roland absentee.
Roland's tummy ache was so bad, he did not attend school, for two days.
This was a normal birthday problem, every year with Roland, Molly like her brother ate too much as well.
Kathy had not realised, that Roland had eaten too much, she just thought that all children, got this problem, now and again, but at this particular birthday Roland ate a lot of cakes, and chocolate biscuits, he also had a box of chocolates he won in the pass the parcel competition, which he also consumed secretly in his bedroom, that Kathy was unaware with,
Kathy had made a lot of food for the other children, not realising that this was not helping the children who could also have been sick later at home. big spread for Roland's birthday and invited a few children from school to his birthday.

CHAPTER 7
SAMMY AND SALLY PLAY IN THE GREEN MEADOW PARK.

After school, and in the school holidays, Sally and Sammy, would play in the Green Meadow Park, this was their favourite park, as it had tall trees, where they could climb to the top, and shout to each other, ' I'm the king of the castle you're a silly rascal,' and secret woods, where they could play, hide and seek, and enjoy skipping, running, cartwheels, or playing ball games, on the grassland areas.

This weekend, Sammy and Sally went as usual, to the park.

When they got there, Sally suggested, they would play hide and seek, she would hide in the woods first, and Sammy, would have to find her.

Sammy agreed, he first faced a tree, to show Sally, she could not see her hide somewhere, then he counted to one hundred slowly saying the numbers to himself, when Sally was convinced that Sammy, was not going to turn around and watch her, she then disappeared.

into the woods.

Eventually Sammy finished counting to one hundred, he shouted, 'Sally I am coming so

But Sammy decided, he find a tree, and maybe see

where Sally had hidden herself, he thought this would be quicker, than running around searching needlessly, he had to find an easy tree to climb, he searched looking around and up lots of tree to find a high tree with wide strong branches making sure they would stand his strength and weight, Sammy eventually found one with the first branch close to the ground, making it easy to start his descent to climb up, he kept climbing until he got as far as he could go, with relief he sat on a wide branch, and made himself comfortable, he looked all around the woods, to watch for any movement in the bushes, with his thoughts Sally could be in a bush, otherwise up a tree, he could also see if she was, as trees are very spacious and open.

'This is fun,' he grinned, 'I can everything going on, I just love being so high up, I wish.

Dad had made us a tree house, that would be great, a string rope ladder, and leave the rest to Sally and me to finish.

In fact, I do see a man coming, he is a long way away, he is wearing a flat hat, his dog looks the dog is taking the man for a walk, by the way he is pulling lead quickly through the woods, thought Sammy, grinning to himself.

He suddenly noticed a bush, moving about, aha-ha is that is where she is hiding, he kept watching the bush for a few minutes, in case it was an animal, he then saw a head bob, up and down, and saw her head appear higher out of the bushes, and then disappear back down again, just to see if Sammy, was coming closer to her hiding place.

Sally, did not know that Sammy, was looking down

on her, from the top of a tree.

While Sammy, was high in the tree, he also saw two of his friends from school, who were driving somewhere, in their car, which was speeding along, heading this way. Sammy tried to wave, to the car, but they did not see him, high in the trees.

The car then disappeared, then Sammy then forgot about them, and now he had found.

Sally's hideout, he could come down, and creep up to the bush, where she was hiding.

He clambered, down the tree carefully, so not to scrape his knees, jumping the remainder of the tree, down, from the last branch with a thump on the hard ground!!

Sammy walked slowly and carefully to where Sally' bush where she was hiding, creping closer and closer, to her bush.

'He moved aside the bush and exposed Sally crouching down on her knees, I can see you.

Sally, admitted Sammy, touching her shoulder, to the elements.

'Oh! She said feeling jumpy 'I did not hear you coming, I was hoping that you would, not find me so quickly,' she admitted, sadly.

I saw Harry and Lloyd, going somewhere, I did wave to them, but they did not see me,' admitted Sammy.

'How did they, see you them in the woods' asked Sally, looking puzzled.

'I saw them up a tree,' said Sammy, smiling.

'Why were you up a tree,' enquired Sally, looking puzzled.

'I went up the tree, because I was bored, with looking for you,' lied Sammy.

'Oh! said Sally, believing his story.

Sammy had got away with his excuses.

'My turn to hide my eyes,' said Sally excited now look for Sammy.

'Okay! said Sammy, bored with all this talk, about the tree hiding himself.

Sally, facing a tree a nearby, and started counting to a hundred, loudly. One two, four still counting eventually to one hundred.

Sammy had run into the woods, after Sally shouted one, and this time, he found a difficult place, to be found.

He spotted a hollow tree, which he disappeared into.

In the meantime, Wayne was driving his two children, in their car, and taking them to their friend's house, to keep the children out of Kathy's way so she could have a sleep. Kathy often took a sleep, so, she would take a nap, in her warm bed, having done her housework, in

the morning. The car passed the park, where the Silverwood children were playing.

Molly announces, 'that Sammy and Sally might be in those woods playing games,'

Wayne Said to the children, do you want to find your friends in the woods and play with them, but the Roland and Molly did not want to get out of the car, it was warm and cosy, all they wanted is to go home and play board games or watch the television.

Wayne was hoping that he could have a quick cigarette while the children were playing with Sally and

Sammy.

'Hurry up Daddy, we want to go home, and try out the new cakes, and biscuits from our favourite shop,' they cried,

'Had you not forgotten later you are seeing your friends, Mathew and Betty,' said Wayne, annoyed with his silly children.

'But Daddy, we want to go home to mummy, and have a nice cake, and our favourite cinnamon and raisons biscuits,' they cried together.

'No! I need to see my friend now, you are going to play with Mathew and Betty, I am close to where my business dealings are,' said Wayne, lying, and feeling angry, with his children

trying to spoil his afternoon treat.

But all Wayne, wanted was to do was to go to the pub, have a beer, and a cigarette, with

Mathew and Betty's father Bill, who also wanted to go down for a beer, and to talk with his friend, Wayne.

Bill's wife was going to work, in the afternoon, to do some private cleaning for an old lady.

The eldest child would look after Roland and Molly, although Betty was more interested, in watching television, then looking after these boring, sister and brother.

Mathew was tough, and talked about football, and Rugby, and only wanted to watch sport, on the television, his sister Betty was also a bit bossy, and not much fun to play with.

They were completely opposite, in interests and hobbies to Roland and Molly, but Wayne was adamant, he was going to the pub, with his friend, Bill. Mathew, wanted to play footie in the garden, but Roland wanted to stay indoors, and watch the television with Betty and Molly, which was not the television programme, that Roland wanted to watch, but Roland just wanted to stay indoors, and listen to the girls, talking although, Molly just sat with Roland, hoping that the television, would be better later, but he was lazy, and liked to sit and keep warm indoors, although it was summer Betty, was not used to playing with girlie children, she was more of a tom boy, and liked playing with boys, and to watch sport, either hockey, or football.

Eventually Wayne came back, and picked up the children, the children loathed, going to the Glade family, as their own father stunk of beer, when he came back, and the children, were frightened of Wayne's driving, it made them scared, he was singing, and not concentrating on the roads, as they drove home, the car would sway back and forth across the roads, missing people, on the pavement, and generally driving dangerously.

In the meantime, Sally had counted to a hundred, and was ready to look for Sammy.

'Coming, shouted Sally, when she had reached a hundred.

'Sammy, where are you?'

She wanders through the woods, she felt very lonely in this dark wood, on her own, what if she sees a man with a dog, would she be scared? Sally looked for ages, Sammy was still hiding in the hollow tree, which was behind the path that Sally was on.

Sammy, was enjoying this hiding, this hollow tree

was cosy and interesting, he watched the ants walking up and down the tree, Sammy thought he could feel safe here, it was like a house snug and warm, and if it rained it would keep him warm and dry, he looked out of his hollow tree and spotted a black bird, high in an oak tree opposite his hollow tree, and because he was quiet, a badger walked past him, outside on the ground was scattered were hundreds of acorns, from the oak tree where the blackbird was sat, while he was in there, chirping away merrily.

Sammy was getting worried, Sally was a long time looking for him, and worried he would never be found.

It was getting dark, and the woods were difficult to see any daylight around him, he was.

getting panicky, Sammy heard Sally, shout, 'Sammy, I cannot find you, and it is getting dark, we should be getting home soon, come out, and give yourself up, you have won the game.

Sammy came out of the tree, and try to remember, where Sally was calling from, I think she is over there he thought.

He started to walk, on the path, that looked familiar.

No sign of Sally, anywhere, Sammy was now getting worried,

'Sally, where are you,' he shouted with a panic voice.

He kept walking, eventually the dark wood, got lighter, much to Sammy's delight, as he nearer to the grassy area of an open field of light.

Sammy looked everywhere, I thought it was Sally, looking for me, so why is she not coming out, so we can get on home,' he said sounding anxious.

Sammy, eventually saw Sally, in the distance, and started to run towards her., he got up to her, and stopped just behind.

'Sally, what are you playing at, you are meant to be looking for me,' moaned Sammy.

'Sorry, Sammy, I got bored with looking for you, and the dark wood scared me. I was.

looking up the tree, and saw a woodpecker at work, pecking the tree, that was fascinating watching and wondering what else he was going to do.

'Were, asked Sammy, now forgotten his problem with Sally looking for him.

'There, in that tree, said Sally, pointing to a massive tree, on the top of the tree was a green woodpecker, tap, tapping on the wood.

'Oh, how exciting,' cried Sammy, with joy.

'It is a big bird, isn't it? Agreed Sally laughing.

'I wish I had a camera; he is so beautiful, big and green, I saw a badger in the wood, and a blackbird,' he bragged.

'Oh, how lucky, said Sally wishing she was there too.

'If you had come looking, for me then you, would have seen it too,' moaned Sammy.

'Can we go, and look for the badger,' asked Sally.

'No, it is getting dark,' said Sammy adamantly, looking down at his watch.

'Mum, said to come home at five o'clock, otherwise, Dad would have to look for us, which is very embarrassing, having your parents calling out, our names in the woods, grumbled Sammy.

'We have a lot to tell Mum and Dad,' admitted Sally,

excited at seeing a woodpecker.

'Yes, and my badger, I saw crawling along in the woods.

'Look Sammy I can see a squirrel dart past me,' squealed Sally with excitement.

'Where? said Sammy, looking for the squirrel,

'You were in front of me, that is why you missed it,' admitted Sally smiling.

'Oh, what was it like then? asked Sammy not believing Sally, and thought she was teasing.

him, for the time he saw a badger and a blackbird.

'Ok! it was grey and had a bushy tail, and it was carrying an acorn in his paws' admitted Sally.

'Then you were right and not fibbing' said Sammy, now believing Sally.

'Yes, told you so,' bragged Sally, sticking her tongue out to Sammy.

'Come on stop be silly Sally, and let's get on home before we get lost in this wood, orders Sammy grumpily.

Sally realises now she just wanted to see Sammy, and is pleased, that they are together Again, and not lost in this dark frightening wood.

Sally holds Sammy's hand and gives it a squeeze pleased they are leaving the woods and are both walking and headed back to their house.

Walking in front of them is Mrs Mason, a neighbour, who lived a few doors from their house, she lived alone, her family who now have gone to live in the North of the country, which are many miles from Mrs Mason house, to be able to help her with her shopping or any other problems she made need help with.

'Is that Mrs Mason,' whispered Sally nudging Sammy.

'Yes! she looks so old, and bent,' admits Sammy whispering, quietly so not that Mrs Mason could not hear them.'

'Those bags look so heavy, she looks like the bags, are going to drag on down on the floor,' said Sally, observing her.

They watched the weight, of the bags drags nearer to the pavement, and Mrs Mason was getting more slower and slower, and more tired, she looked like she was dropping with the bags, onto the pavement.

Sally looked at Sammy, and whispered,

'Shall we help her home, then she will get back, and have a sit down. she does look so slow, and tired 'admitted Sally.

They came up to Mrs Mason, slowly not to startle her.

'Mrs Mason, can we help you,' asked Sally, who had stopped close to Mrs Mason, and she was so bent over with her shopping, she had to put down the shopping on the pavement, to stand up right to see who was calling her name.

'Oh, hello young Sally,' she said.

Sammy arrived near Mrs Mason later.

'Is this Sammy,' she asked, looking at Sammy through her glasses, which had slid down her nose, almost coming off the end of it.

She remembered that they both had a S name each.

'Yes,' said Sammy, looking at Mrs Mason, who had red hands because she had been carrying a heavy bag, for a quite a long time, that made her hands hot and sweaty.

'Can we carry your bags for you,' Mrs Mason, we noticed you have heavy bags' asked Sammy sympathetically.

'I should say no, but these were so heavy that my arms, are feeling like they were going to drop off, and I have eggs in the bag, 'we know what happens, if they fall on the floor' admitted Mrs Mason.

'Yes,' said Sally, nodding her head.

Sammy picked up one of her shopping bags, from the ground, and Sally, picked up another bag, from her other arm.

'Well, 'what are you two, doing out so late, it is getting dark, and your parents might worry about you,' asked Mrs Mason, sternly.

'Don't worry, Mrs Mason, we are on the way home, we will help you, with the bags, and then we will both head home,' said Sammy reassuring Mrs Mason.

Sally and Sammy, took hold of her shopping bags, and walked together, towards Mrs.

Mason's house they took them, into the house, and carefully put the foods, and the eggs, on the table, so, Mrs Mason, could put them away, when she had made herself a cup of tea, and a sit down.

'Thank you, Sally and Samuel, for helping me with the shopping,' said Mrs Mason, smiling at the two children.

Sally, giggled to herself, about the Samuel name, which Mrs Mason, said about Sammy.

But Sammy, heard her say that, and realised she was getting old, and had forgotten his proper name.

Mrs Mason, sat on her chair in the kitchen, glad to have help, with her heavy shopping bags.

Can we put the kettle on for you? Asked Sally, hoping she would say yes.

'Thank you, Sara,' said Mrs Mason sitting on a chair, and pointing to the kettle.

Sally filled the kettle up with water from the tap and went over to put the kettle on.

'Thank you, Sarah,' said Mrs Mason, looking happier and rested sitting on a chair and

relieved she was home, and not carrying those heavy bags.

Sammy and Sally, we are going now Mrs Mason.

'Goodbye Mrs Mason,' said Sammy, smiling at her.

'Bye, Mrs Mason,' said Sally.

'Bye you too,' shouted Mrs Mason.

They got Mrs Mason front door and came out and shut it quietly.

They arrived home, and settled in with their homework, they had their supper, and eventually went to bed.

CHAPTER 8
THE SILVERTONS GO TO TEA WITH THE BROOME FAMILY.

Nearly every other Sunday, the Silverwood family were invited to The Broome family for tea at three, had to be three o'clock in their house unless they went out, so that their children could play with the Roland and Molly. Laura liked Kathy's company, but she did not find her, always on her wave length, but Laura was a tolerant and kind person, and hoped she could help Kathy, but she did not know how, and Steve her husband, also found Wayne, the children's father, not someone, he could take out, to meet his friends, possibly because Steve did not smoke, or drink beer.

But they all still went over, and sometimes as a thank you Laura would give Kathy a jar of, her homemade marmalade, as a treat for her, this was her special marmalade, made with alcohol.

Laura had Brandy in her food cupboard which was handy for her cooking certain cakes and Marmalades, her speciality was oranges, soaked in this Brandy, and made this into her special marmalade, only given to adults, because of its alcohol ingredients, she would remind Kathy, on no account, to give this to your children, this is an adult marmalade, for you and Wayne only.

Laura and Steve were already waiting, for Sally and

Sammy to get their shoes on, to go out.

'Come on Sally,' urges Sammy, trying to rush Sally, to get her shoes on as they are both waiting to go out, to see the Broome families.

'What is your problem?' moaned Sally, putting her shoes on quickly, because of Sammy insistent to rushing her.

'I want to go to Roland's house, but I do not want to go,' moans Sammy.

'If you do not want to go, then why are you are hurrying me up?' asks Sally, annoyed at being rushed so quickly.

'That is right, the sooner, we go the sooner we come back home, I really loathe the Broome's house,' moaned Sammy.

'Maybe next week, we may not go again,' reassured Sally.

'Why do you say that? inquired Sammy, standing patiently, watching Sally, who had sat on the bottom of the stairs getting her shoes on.

'I just feel things are going to be different, somehow,' said Sally, having a strange thought.

'Oh! said Sammy, looking very puzzled at Sally thinking's.

'Are you to ready to go to the Broome's family? Asks Laura.

'Yes, I am ready, but Sammy does not want to go,' informs Sally.

'I know Sammy, hates going, but one day we may not go,' said Laura, reassuring.

'What is it with you two, why are you two keeps telling me the same news, one day we might not be going to their house again, are they are moving away or something? Asks Sammy very puzzled by the same answers.

Sammy has no idea, into Mum and Sally reckoning, but he said no more on the subject.

They all got to the car, this time Steve was driving, much to Laura's relief.

Laura sat next to Steve in the passenger seat, with the children at the back of the car, and they head for the Broome's family home.

Eventually, they arrive at the Broome's house, their house has outside parking, so Steve finds that when they get to the house, the space outside the house is always occupied with a van, so, Steve finds must find a space further down the road.

Steve is the first, to get out of the car, followed by Laura, Sally, and then Sammy who was dawdling.

They walk along the pavement, eventually arriving at the gate of the house, Laura and Steve reach the front door, first, with Sammy and Sally behind them, both reluctant to go.

Laura rings the bell.

They hear footsteps, coming to the door, the door opens, and Kathy stands there, wearing a pretty cotton dress, with her apron with two large pockets, she stands there, with her hands in her apron pockets, not expecting them yet, but happy to see them early than later.

'Hello everyone, come on in, Roland is upstairs, Molly is in the sitting room, and Wayne is.

outside in the garage, checking some tools for a job, next week, but come in, and we can wait for Wayne later.

They all march in, Sammy goes upstairs, and the rest

of the family, follow Kathy into the sitting room.

Today, is no different than any other Sunday, with the Broome family.

Kathy, only always gives the Silverwood family bought cakes, filled with jam and cream, and have cinnamon, and ginger biscuits, the Silverwood children love those biscuits.

The rest of the Silverwood family did not want to go into the Broome household, as Steve is not familiar with Wayne lifestyle, all Wayne wanted to talk about is Television, and board games, he reads trash newspapers, and likes indoor interests.

Steve only drinks tea, coffee, and fruit juices, he sometimes enjoyed a glass of wine, but

never touches beer, and on occasions might have a port, and Laura would have a sweet white wine, and only have one small glass, when she went goes out socially.

Kathy only has one good friend, which is Laura.

Kathy talks with people at the school gates, but no one wants to ask Kathy to tea or socially, her only conversations with Laura are talking about are food, and pop music.

Whereas Laura, has a vast number of friends, who like herself, enjoyed talking about politics, books, and radio four programmes.

But Laura, is a tolerate and patient person, and goes along with Kathy's interests.

Laura decided to talk about cooking, and popular music, not that she knew much, about this Kind of music, she like classical music, especially solo violins, and orchestral music.

As Kathy, eats a lot of greasy foods, chips and

sausages, her face is suffered with oily spots, and she has blood shot eyes and dark rims under her eyes, her teeth, are neglected, she does always clean her teeth every night, she enjoys her sweet puddings, and piled them on her.

plate, and eats cakes, and biscuits every day.

The Broome family did not like fruit, as it wasn't as sweet as chocolate, or sugary sweets.

Molly and Roland, always to stay in, and played board games, jigsaw puzzles, and watched television, and they always stayed up late, as Kathy and Wayne like a drink and fell asleep in front of the television, so Roland and Molly, do not have any discipline, to go to bed early, waited to be told to go to bed, when Kathy and Wayne wake up from their drunken state.

Kathy also liked staying in her house, as much as possible, she kept her house hot, and very stuffy, no windows opened, as this would make her family cold, and they all felt the cold, having sat down all day, and not moving about enough.

Kathy had her favourite seat, having always sat in her armchair, it had a big dent in it, and she would be the only one who could sit in it, other people must sit on the sofa, next to the Roland and Molly, and they all looked like a row of peas, with Wayne at one end and the Silverwood family at the other end.

The Silverwood family did not like Kathy's hot stuffy house, and often felt ill from all the heat, they wanted to get some fresh cool air, when they came home, they mouth felt dry, and were very thirsty from the hot airless house.

Also, The Broome family, never enjoyed being in

The Silverwood house, which was fresh, cool and their house had a fresh air aroma about it, having opened the windows, with weather permitting, they also had a bonus of the smell of fresh air from their grass cuttings, and the woods nearby.

When the Broome family, came over to the Silverwood house, they huddled themselves next to the radiators, hoping to keep warm, but this was turned off in the summer days, which was would have been an unnecessary waste of heating if left on, as most of the time they were outside in the garden or in the park.

Every day poor Kathy was always tired, even though she had an afternoon nap, when her husband was out, or working, and the children were watching a long television programme, or at school.

This annoyed the Silverwood children, all they wanted to do was play outdoors in the fresh air, and their sleep was always good, as they would wake up feeling fresh and ready to carry on. They were good at sports and were keen on getting good speeds for running.

But the Silverwood family were easy going, and did not mind for the sake of peace, to stay in and play indoor games with the Broome family.

But the youngest child Molly was annoyed with the Silverwood family, they were happy, full of energy, and slim, Molly always wanted to thin, so when they came to tea, Molly would pile on the cakes and biscuits, on Sally and Sammy, you must try this cake that Mum made,' said Molly, being kind but had an ulterior motive.

'Thank you,' said Sally, but what about you Sammy, we have plenty, said Molly, smiling with a cunning smile. Neither they realised what Molly was doing, they just thought she was kind and generous.

But two months later, after going for these fattening teas, the children started to get bad.

marks at school. They found sleeping difficult, and getting up for school, completely impossible.

Sammy soon became bad at Maths, and when it came to the summer games, could not run fast. Steve Silverwood was upset for his children, and asked Laura.

'What shall we do, the children are ill, and slow at schoolwork, why do you think Steve?

It started when, we were going to the Broome house, every Sunday instead of once a month,' Mentioned Laura, looking very anxious, where her children acting like the Broome children?

'We must stop going there,' replied Steve adamantly.

'Yes, I must agree,' admitted Laura.

'But how can we tell them, this is their fault., said Steve.

'Why don't we get them over here, but they do not like our house it is cold, and we always have the window open with fresh air. I will make them something in between healthy, and not healthy, and maybe it may be the answer.

Laura normally makes cakes, using her best ingredients, without the added preservatives, and colouring, whereas Kathy always bought cakes from the shops.

CHAPTER 9
THE RAINBOW CAKE

Sammy, The Broome family are coming to tea on Sunday, I will be given them our rainbow cake, that Kathy likes so much,' announces Laura.

'Oh, no Mum, they are full of artificial colouring, you know that will make me, come out in an itchy rash,' admitted Sammy, sadly.

' No, darling this is my recipe, I am using fresh fruit and vegetables, but I will be mimicking this cake, so we can disguise that the cake, is the healthy one which is full of good vitamins, and minerals, and Kathy will have a healthy cake, this one is kind, for her body, for a change, then the bought cakes she always buys,' announced Laura.

'Thanks mum,' Phew! I am relieved' said Sammy, now happy, with Mum explanation.

Laura goes ahead, and makes the cake, adding the fruit and vegetables, she enjoyed the challenge to mimic the cake, that Kathy always raved about.

Lau starts her cake by making four mixtures, of a Victorian cake, putting them into four bowls, with the dark beetroot colour of the red colouring, she first cooks the beetroot until it is soft, she then mashed the beetroot until it pulped, the second colour being the yellow, being the lemon, just juice and cooked apple, the third mixture of carrot juice, orange colour, she cooks carrots, and then mashed into a pulp, the forth is green colour, a fruit a summer field apple, also cooked mashed and then into a pulp, she mixed each one, separately. Laura, then had four separates colour mixtures, each one she put in a flan tin, cooks for twenty minutes, cooled. She then put the layers on top of each other, on the plate, with a paper doily underneath, and then sandwiched together, starting with the beetroot-coloured cake, followed by the lemon, then orange one, and finally the green apple one, between each layer, she put a homemade, confectioner cream.

To finish the cake, Laura put a thin layer of cream cheese, all over the cake, and then.

sprinkled the cake with hundreds and thousands, and then she called the two children down, to inspect her rainbow cake.

They both arrived in the kitchen and come over to Laura who smiling at her beautiful achieve of her rainbow cake.

'Now Sally and Sammy, what do you think of my cake,' enquires Laura grinning with excitement of her new creation.

'OH, lovely Mum! said Sally smiling, with a look, can I lick the bowl, of cream cheese.

'Oh, thank you, no more rashes with this cake, Mum,' admitted Sammy. grinning.

'No, and I am sure I will make this again soon.

'Oh, by the way, asked Laura to Sally and Sammy, this is a bought cake.

'But you made it mum,' said Sally looking puzzled.

'Yes, but this is a secret from Kathy, Sally, I will explain later,' said Laura.

'Okay, mum! said Sally, wondering what her Mum was thinking about making her children lie, looking puzzled but did not ask any more questions about the cake, just accepted mum explanation. Sally and she left the kitchen.

Sammy stayed alone with Mum and waited for Sally to leave the kitchen.

'Wow! mum, you are wonderful, they will never know, unless Sally forgets and says something about the cake, admitted Sammy.

'Yes, I will look silly, if this goes wrong', admits Laura.

'No, we will keep this the Silverton's family secret, for now maybe one day, I will divulge the whereabout of secret of our cake.

'Kathy and Wayne, always looking forward to any Sunday treat, and to spend time with the Silverton's family, they thought this family, were someone to be seen with, the other parents thought that they were good parents too, their children were always were well mannered, kind, to their children, and the parents were good role models.

But Kathy did not know, Laura was going to make a cake with vegetables and fruit, chopped up and cooked in this cake.

On the Sunday as promised, the house was not any warmer, if it was when they arrived.

they were wearing to many clothes on, they thought it was warm, but with all the cooking,

Laura had done today, it did make the house warmer than usual, by the evening it would have cooled down anyway.

Eventually the Broome family arrived and sat down hoping for a hot house with lots of cakes from their favourite cake shops.

'What a lovely warm house,' remarked Kathy.

'Yes, it is, the heating is warming up nicely,' lied Laura.

'I love the smell of your house,' commented Kathy.

'Yes, thank you,' said Laura, smiling to herself.

'I want you, to try this cake we bought from the shop,' said Laura. leaving the room.

Laura went into the kitchen, and bought out her home-made cake, she had already, put on a plate, cut it so, it looked even all around, so it did not have the home-made look, which sometimes it has risen in the middle, but that had been made by an amateur baker.

'That looks strange,' said Kathy, looking puzzled as her bought cake, that did not have beetroot dotted in the cake.

'Yes, the rainbow cake from Inspirational cakes and co,' said Laura lying again.

Kathy had a cake beside her, she was thinking to herself, *what a strange colour, it must be the colouring they use.*

Everything went okay, the family loved the cake, and bought ones which Laura had bought from the shop which were cinnamon and ginger biscuits.

Laura told them again that they were shop bought, she was just reassuring Kathy that the cake was bought, which of course was far from the truth.

Steve was left with Wayne talking about golf, and Laura talked about cooking, using nuts, carrots, just to reassure Kathy that these could be used in cakes, and sometimes fruit, not only dried fruit, and sometimes fresh fruit.

Laura was pleased that Kathy, was eating at her *home-made home cake* and she was happy, she got away with her white lie cake.

The children played indoor golf, in the garage, and Sammy taught Roland and Molly juggling and How to play skittles, with their plastic skittle bowls with a wooden ball, all that toeing, and froing made Roland puff and pant, but Sammy was glad to see Roland doing some exercises, and sweating.

The house was warm, Roland did not feel cold, with all the running about, with the skittles and playing indoor golf. But Laura had secretly opened just one window,

They all had a lovely time, and eventually went home, much to the relief of her lying day with the Broome family.

The next day Kathy came over to see Kathy, and said last night our children were very tired and wanted to go in bed early, and not watch television, but when they got up, they were full of energy, they felt that they wanted to do something energetic and sporty. Exercising, eating healthier, and enjoy being outside getting fresh air and sunshine bathing on their skins, making them have an appetite and being tired not interested in watching television, but playing with a ball against the wall.

CHAPTER 10
THE CONFESSION

'I asked Kathy to come for a walk with us this afternoon, our children will take them for a nature walk, and then we will go from there,' smiled Laura, to Steve one morning at breakfast time.

'Good idea darling, that is kind of you, good luck I hope Kathy appreciates what you are doing for them,' says Steve, giving his wife a kiss.

Laura and her two children picked up three of the Broome's family, one Saturday afternoon, and took them to a small park with a beautiful lake there, the six of them walked around the perimeter of this park.

The park was a short walk away from Laura's house.

Roland grumbled all the time, Molly and Sally just talked non-stop about boys and didn't 'notice the walk, they just enjoyed each other company. Sammy was just happy walking behind Kathy and his Mother, listening to their conversation, which he really enjoyed, about.

Laura's telling Kathy about job in London.

They all came back for a cup of tea and a biscuit, the children all played in the house, to please Roland and Molly, since they had their walk, and was pleased to sit down and play board games, which please Roland he was glad to rest, and he stopped grumbling then much to

Sammy's relief Laura gave the children some chocolate biscuits and lemonade, a piece of orange and a straw, in their glass of lemonade.

Laura and Kathy talked about carrots cake, and beetroot being added to some of her cakes and how she makes raspberry trifle.

While they were sitting down having a chat and a cup of tea.

Laura confessed to Kathy, about her Rainbow cake.

'Kathy, I went to the Inspirable shop to buy the Rainbow cake, and they have stopped making that cake, four months ago, she was telling Kathy about the rainbow cake.

'Laura where did you get the cake from then?' asked Kathy.

'I had to make one instead, I made it as good as they make them in the shops, I am sorry Kathy to deceive you, I hope you did not mind, 'said Laura lying.

'No, I really enjoyed it, my children had a good night sleep, and Wayne had a good sleep too, he always grumbled, that he had a headache after, my bought cakes, I never thought it was the cakes' fault,' admitted Kathy.

'It would be the cake, it has chemicals in the cake,' informed Laura.

What chemicals? asks Kathy, with a raised eyebrow.

They have chemicals in cakes, biscuits, and preservatives to keep them fresh, otherwise they get mouldy, and dry,' informed Laura.

Oh? I did not know that I just thought it was what we normally use, margarine, flour, sugar and eggs,' said a puzzled Kathy.

'No, next time you buy a cake, read the label on the packet, it will have names not even.

Wayne could pronounce,' said Laura., showing Kathy, where to find the label, she had some biscuits which she had bought that day, it has fewer ingredients than some other biscuits, and cakes.

'Oh, I am glad you pointed them out to me, I would have never known, I see from your biscuits, that everything has some extra ingredients, that we never knew existed how terrible. Said Kathy rather annoyed and puzzled too.

'Yes, cooking cakes yourself, much better, you could save your family, from all the chemicals in the cakes' admitted Laura hopefully.

'I will look for those strange names, on the back of my food, from now on,' admitted Kathy

Laura took Kathy, Roland, and Molly home, after they had asked to go soon, as Wayne need to have his food, quickly after he gets home, he gets grumpy when he arrives home, and Kathy need to feed him quickly before he loses his temper with the children.

Kathy went out the next day, after what Laura said about chemicals, and went into town, and picked up a packet of chocolate, snip snaps, and on the back of the packet, was the word Missandel.

What on earth is that mean? she went over to the counter, and asked what this word was meant to be? Miss, she asked the assistant at the counter.

The assistant behind the counter, looked at the packet that Kathy had given her, she put on her glasses, and said, 'well I do not know, some sort of preservative possibly.

'But why are they there? she asked her.

Madam, to make sure they do not go mouldy' he replies.

'Oh! said Kathy,

She put the packet back on the shelf and walked out.

'I am not buying those again, she muttered to herself.

The same day she told Wayne about her find in the biscuits; Wayne reply was:

'I will eat any biscuits; I am not fussed about chemicals' he said.

'I will not buy them again; I will make some biscuits and you will eat my biscuits grumbled Kathy.

Wayne grunted and walked outside to have a cigarette.

'Those cigarettes are bad for you,' shouted Kathy.

'For goodness's sake Kath ever since you went to tea with Laura yesterday, you are moaning.

to me about my habits, drinking smoking, and eating cakes, I do not want you to see that woman again,' shouted Wayne.

Kathy, said no more to Wayne, she just sat on the sofa and switched on the television and put her feet up on the pouffe.

CHAPTER 11
THE UNEXPECTED PHONE CALL

One Monday morning, after Laura had dropped the children off to school, and Steve had caught the train to work, Laura, was settling down in her kitchen, with a well-deserved cup of tea, and a plate of her favourite chocolate biscuits, she was just having her second biscuit, her one luxury, she gave herself this one for spoiling herself, when she has done her chores, she had made a list of jobs, to do that day, which were cooking, and cleaning, Laura looks around the kitchen, and wondered, what do I need to clean the house, hmm, I will start after, I have finished my tea, I will take the vacuum cleaner out, and then I will start on cooking some apples, for an apple pie, while she was deep in thought, the phone started to ring.

'I wonder who that can be, so early in the morning, I am not expecting anyone, I just hope it is not someone, who wants to sell me some double-glazed windows.

She got up, and walks over to the phone, which is on the other side of the kitchen, she

stretches over to reach the phone, she looks down at the memory plate, and sees it displays Kathy and Wayne telephone number, what on earth does, Kathy want, it can't be Wayne he is meant to beat work, or is he? this is a quite unexpected phone call, from the Broome household, this time of day, she knew that Wayne never phones her, so it must be Kathy.

Laura answers it, quietly, and slightly worried.

'Hello,' she asked hesitantly.

Laura felt that something must be wrong, maybe I am just thinking how unusual, she was apprehensive, on this sudden phone call from Kathy. I saw Kathy this morning, she could have spoken to me, at the school gates, saving herself a phone call, but thinking back, she did not see Kathy, or any of her children at school, which was very unusual.

'Are you there Laura? asked Kathy, sounding very anxious.

'Yes, I am here Kathy are you alright? 'replies Laura, trying to reassure her.

Laura is picking up, on Kathy upsetting voice.

'No, Laura, I am very worried, something has happened to Wayne,' she said frantically.

'What has happened to Wayne? Enquired Laura, anxiously, now getting the vibes of a worried friend.

Laura has always worries about the Broome family, and their unhealthy life style, half expecting Kathy, to say that Wayne, has had a heart attack or worse.

Kathy sounded fretful and very stressed.

'Wayne's knee has swollen up, and he cannot walk, he is in terrible pain, he tossed and turned all night long, I have never heard, such a groaning from him before. We could not take the children to school this morning, they did not mind, they haven't got a clue about.

Wayne and his knee, they just thought he had drunk

too much, and was still asleep. He is still in bed, and in too much pain, to move to go to work.

'Kathy, I am so sorry to hear, is there anything, I can do for you? asks Laura, sympathetically.

' No, thank you , Laura, he has had this problem, for a few years, and the doctor told him that he needs a new knee replacement, if he lost a lot of weight, then his knee would recover on its own, but Wayne being Wayne, refused to lose weight, or stop drinking beer, or smoking, he still loves eating big meals, but I do not know, what to give him, I was brought up, with what I was given myself, I know nothing about, what my family should eat, . I am in such a dilemma, it must be my fault, he has this problem, giving him foods, that makes him fat, if he did not drink beer, maybe he would not be so big, if he goes to hospital, it must be the hospital, which is hundreds, of miles ways, but with this hospital, he will be not able to come home, till after the operation, he is going to be away for six weeks, with having to learn to walk again, he is so overweight, so he really needs to lose weight, and if he comes home, he will be lazy, and eat the wrong foods, maybe he may, then he might, not need a hip replacement,' admitted Kathy, sounding very despondent.

Laura, thought that Kathy, sounded so worried, while she was telling her everything, she was thinking what she could do for her.

Laura, just waited to hear, what Kathy wanted her to do.

'So, what are you going to do? Asked Laura.

She wanted to respond to her friend's needs, Laura,

was thinking poor Kathy, she relies, on her Wayne for everything, although he is an unhealthy man, he did pay for all the bills, and Kathy, has never learnt to pay, a bill in her life, this is a big shock, she got unfortunately married straight from home, where her parents looked her and Kathy's brother Kenny, all of Kathy's life, she left home young, and never had to defend for herself.

But Kathy's brother married a woman, who was very good with home management, which helped him learnt about those sorts of things.

Kathy met Wayne when he did a few odd jobs for Kathy's family, when he was home, being a long-distance lorry drive, and to make Wayne marry her, she told him she was pregnant.

So, Wayne married Kathy, thinking that Kathy was pregnant, he married her at the young age of nineteen, but after they had married, she admitted she was not pregnant, she could not bear him being away from her, she missed him so much, as he was long-distance lorry driver, going away for long times. When he came home, his father was a builder, so Wayne took odd jobs with his father. But when he was away, he picked up bad habits in greasy cafes on route...

He married Kathy and stayed in his hometown, and had a rented house, doing odd jobs with a builder, when he felt like it.

Kathy told Laura, she rang the doctor this morning, and the receptionist told me, that she would get back to me. When she did get back to me, she said Mr Broome, must have the operation straight away. But they can only do it, on the following Tuesday. I have rung.

Chloe and Louie, Wayne's cousins, about Wayne, and they said they have not seen Wayne for ages, and this would be a good opportunity to see him, they admitted that the last time, they saw Wayne he looked overweight and ill and both, are into healthy living, and quietly admitted to Kathy that they would be kind and firm to Wayne, making sure he was fed well, and helped with his exercises, , . I am relieved about this, I can let someone else look after Wayne, and maybe they can get him fit and well again.

Our doctor will order an ambulance, he will then be taken to the Hospital, and Wayne will then have op, afterwards back to Chloe and Louie they will go up to the Hospital, take him back to their house, and look after Wayne, and give him good food, and exercises, they are good cousins, Chloe and Louie, who live in this area, they will help poor Wayne, and keep an eye on him, Louie is a fitness coach, so he will help him, as well as with the physio. Chloe will see to his diet, they have offered to put him up, until he loses the weight. In the meantime, I have no car, to take the children to school, the car must have a MOT, and it has been a problem with me sometimes, Wayne has admitted it has a brake problem, and other small.

things, like a new tyre, I did not know this, when I take the children to school, Wayne is so drunk sometimes, he is unaware of this problem,' sighed Kathy.

'But Kathy the school is so close, they could walk to school,' admitted Laura, astonished about having, to make the children, in a car when they could easily walk.

'I cannot expect my children, to walk to school, they

do not walk, Roland would refuse to go to school, admitted Kathy, tapping her fingers on the table.

'Well', Kathy they are meant to go to school, it is compulsory to go to school, you will be fined, and maybe sent to prison, if you do not get them to school, you will mark my words,' moaned Laura angrily with Kathy spoiling their children, she raised her eyebrows with amazement.

'Oh, I suppose so,' sighed Kathy feeling confused and upset.

Laura added,' Steve and I can help you with the shopping, you will get a lift, but the rest will be up to you, I will help you, with making meals, if this will save you money, and teach you things that Wayne has not taught you, electric bills, etc, while Wayne is away, you will cope.

with fewer meals, you will have to discipline the children, and they will be glad not to have a Dad, who drinks, my children have mentioned, that Wayne drunk to much beer, the car stunk of beer, and Molly worries, that his driving is very scary, when he drives them to school in the morning, he speeds, and going around the corners very fast. Making them frightened that the car would crash,' admitted Laura, sadly.

'Yes, that is true,' agreed Kathy.

'When Wayne has gone to Hospital, we need a plan of action,' Laura, said, confidently.

'Thanks Laura you are an angel,' said Kathy, feeling better knowing, she had support on this terrible day.

'No Kathy just a friend,' admitted Laura smiling.

Kathy, put the phone down, and had a quiet weep,

wiped her eyes, and went back to the family, where Molly, noticed that her mum had been crying.

'What is wrong mum,' asked Molly, coming up to her Mum, to give her a hug.

'Nothing, I have been talking to Laura, and she said she would support me, while your Dad is away. We will have to stay at home, until Daddy goes into hospital, I cannot leave him in this state, you will walk to school, as Daddy won't be driving you, until he gets back from Hospital, and that might not be for at least two months, so I will walk with you, and Roland to school.

'Mum I cannot possibly walk to school, I will not go,' moaned Roland. Sadly.

'I cannot go either,' admitted Molly.

'Molly it is compulsory to go to school, Mummy will go to prison if you don't go.

We must all walk together, we will walk slowly, and Laura is going to help me, make cheap new meals, and Laura is here, if you need any other help,' said Kathy reminding the two children.

'Okay, said Molly, making a disgruntled face, at Roland.

Roland looked at Molly, with a grimace face.

That Tuesday, Wayne, was due to leave for the hospital, several miles away, he had his small suitcase ready for his trip, the ambulance arrived, with two paramedics, they checked he was Wayne Broome, his age and his right address was his, and when they had the right man, they helped him, with his suitcase, they went back to the ambulance, and came in with a wheelchair to the house, the two men helped him onto the wheelchair,

Wayne plonked himself with the help of Eric, the tall paramedic, sat in the waited to leave the house.

The Paramedic, told the family that Wayne, would be in the ambulance about an hour and half, and would be escorted to the Hospital, where he would be put in Highwood ward, The Hospital Hockfield, for a knee replacement.

'I will not be able to come to the hospital, said Kathy, to two paramedic men, but my cousin.

Louie will be coming to the Hospital, instead of me, and keep an eye on him, Wayne, he will be looked after by Chloe and Louie after the operation, he will stay with them, and recuperate afterwards.,' announced Kathy.

When all the formalities had been sorted, Wayne was wheeled outside, by the two a paramedic's Eric, and Andy.

Kathy, Molly and Roland followed, Wayne who sat in wheelchair looking sorrowful and sad at leaving his family, while he was wheeled out, she watched him being boarded onto the ambulance, waiting at the doorway, as Wayne boarded the ambulance, as was helped on the ambulance, by Eric and Andy.

The family watched their Dad, board the ambulance, Molly got hold of her mum's hand, and squeezed it, Molly looks up at Kathy, making sure Kathy was staying too, she was now feeling very insecure, as one of her parents, were leaving for the first time, since she was born.

Roland also was there watching the ambulance men take his Dad, he stood away from both of Kathy and Molly, he now felt the man of the family. Wayne looked sad and pathetic as he was wheeled onto the lift shaft, and it moves up level with ambulance, then pushed into the ambulance, Wayne turned around to Kathy, and waved gently goodbye. looking forlorn and freighted.

Kathy waved back, he then disappeared, behind the doors, with Eric, Andy then shut the Ambulance door tightly, and got in the driving seat, then the ambulance whizzed down the road disappearing into the busy traffic.

Kathy, and Molly both stood weeping, Roland just stood, amazed of the Ambulance, which he had never seen before parked outside his house, he noticed the whole street coming out, or peeping behind their curtains, probably wondering why, Wayne, was taken away in an ambulance.

Kathy, and the children returned into the house, before any neighbours, asked them any questions about Wayne.

After Wayne had gone, Kathy was in no state, to take the children to school, they just sat in front of the television, while Kathy went upstairs, and lay on the bed crying.

CHAPTER 12
A NEW START FOR THE BROOME FAMILY

The next day was different, there was no one to take the children to school. Wayne occasionally took the children, leaving them at the school gates to make their own way there. He would do this on his way to work, in his old works van.

Kathy was awake early, as she saw no point in staying in bed due to fact, she was worried about Wayne, she had tossed and turned all night, as she was now awake, she came downstairs, and went into the kitchen, and made herself a cup of coffee and sat down.

Molly wandered into the kitchen, about an hour later, and saw Kathy sitting with her untouched coffee, clutching a cold and tasteless drink.

Kathy was still in shock, not having her husband there, he was always home these, never away from the family. This was strange for Kathy, but not for the children who were not as worried as Kathy was about Wayne, their Mum was always there, to look after them, their

Dad, was not a stable man, who was always drinking, and being drunk, but Mum knew she

had to be stable one in the family, on occasion drunk with Wayne before going to bed. As the children were around mostly watching Kathy from getting drunk as much as her husband, she could see that Wayne could sleep it off. But luckily Kathy had a sleep in the afternoon, mostly because of Wayne keeping her awake at night with his extremely loud snoring noises.

Kathy just sat just staring at the wall, of a poster of white horses riding across the beach.

Molly came over to Kathy and looked at her she stared at her sad face.

'Mum! can I have toast and jam for breakfast,' asked Molly, looking at her Mum for a responsive reply.

Kathy did not respond, as she was still staring at the poster.

Molly shook her Mum, on her arm.

Kathy looked up and looked at straight through at Molly.

'Molly it is you, responded Kathy, still dazed, and in shock.

'Mum, can I have toast and jam for breakfast,' asked Molly repeating herself again.

Roland stormed into the kitchen and sat down at the table abruptly expecting to be waited on and to be given his breakfast as usual.

Molly looked across to Roland.

'I think Mum isn't happy, as Dad has gone away, so, Roland you will have to get your own breakfast, I am having toast, and Mum will probably get my toast, as it is dangerous for

me to use the toaster,' explained Molly, knowing Kathy, would get her toast as she might burn herself trying.

'Oh, said Roland, shocked at what Molly had just told him to do.

Kathy was aware of the two children, being there.

She eventually announced, to Roland and Molly, 'we need to leave early, as we are going to walk to school today.

The thought of walking to school, was not in Roland's regime, he was adamant, he had decided, he was not going to walk to school, so he came up with an excuse.

'Mum, I do not feel well,' moaned Roland, faking his illness.

Kathy responded by saying, 'Why are you feeling ill? she stated at Roland annoyed with

him, when all she wanted of today, for everything to work out normally, without her.

children trying to make her life difficult today, after having a bad night, and missing me.

husband, she was hoping to go to Laura's and have a shoulder to cry on, as she would be a

good support to her on this terrible day.

'I have a tummy ache,' moans Roland, rubbing his tummy, and looking very sorry for himself.

'You were alright yesterday,' remarked Kathy, looking at Roland with contempt.

She came over to Roland to feel his forehead for a temperature.

She touched his forehead, with the palm of her hand.

'You feel warm, and completely normal, she said, trying to reassure him.

She stared at Roland, to see how ill he was, or if he

was pretending to be ill.

Roland looked down at the floor, hoping for some sympathy, and thinking about another excuse not to walk to school, and maybe he could get out of this going to school now he had to walk.

'You must go to school, it is compulsory to go, I am seeing Laura later for a cookery lesson, she will not be happy if I cancel my lesson with her.' ordered Kathy, getting angry at

Roland for trying to spoil her day, she was feeling upset, and annoyed with Wayne for making himself, have a bad knee and leaving her with all the problems of the house, their children and like paying household bills alone.

Kathy looked again at Roland's face; he still had a sorrowful face.

Kathy, was not having any more of Roland's excuses, she did not care if Roland was ill, she was going to Laura to have some cookery lessons, and to talk, to someone who has a sympathetic ear, and maybe learn something new for supper, she liked Laura, and was

quite in awe of her knowledge, and her lovely family, they were always nice children, who were never ill, or difficult to manage.

'Roland gets ready now, 'go upstairs immediately she said, shouting at Roland.

Roland looked at his mother's angry face and did not argue.

He quickly ran upstairs, and got dressed, and quickly came downstairs again.

'Now Roland, today you can have cornflakes with

one teaspoonful of sugar, I think we need to rethink your food intake, I do not want you want you ending like your Dad, fat and in need of a knee replacement.

Kathy got the cornflakes out on a bowl, giving him one teaspoon of sugar and some milk, and handing it to Roland who looked at his sorrowful small bowl of cornflakes.

Roland ate his cornflakes solemnly, and quietly.

Kathy also did Molly's toast making sure her toast just a small amount of butter and jam, and giving it to Molly, who looked sad and despondent at Kathy sad face, and missing her Dad too.

Molly ate her toast, she was not enjoying this toast, as she had lost her appetite, feeling sad at her Mother sadness.

They both were subdued, and they were not happy with walking to school, but they did not want their mother going to prison and having to some stranger's home to live.

After then had finished their breakfast, no go upstairs and get your teeth brushed and come.

down today we have no choice, our car has no MOT, which means that your Dad, did not take it to a garage, to get it fixed, and we may have an accident, if we drive it in that condition, and end up in hospital too, and Dad's van is only insured for him to drive, so the van is out of the question.

They both ran upstairs obediently.

When they had brushed their teeth, Roland came down first, and stood upright at the bottom of the stairs, waiting for his next command from Kathy.

Molly came down next, she hurriedly put on her coat, while standing next to Roland.4

'Good, now let's go, outside you two, they all went outside, then Kathy slammed the door,

And walked down the road, with Kathy behind them, the two children marched down the road going to school grudgingly.

They arrived earlier than usual and went into the school.

'Off you go,' commanded, Kathy.

Roland and Molly, said goodbye to Kathy, they both walked away from her, Roland turned around looking at Kathy, still with a sad face, hoping to get some sympathy, from Kathy.

But Kathy had already left and wanted to get home, and ring Laura, and did not see.

Roland, she walks quickly home, she eventually arrived back, and rang Laura as soon as she got in.

Laura, said to Kathy, give me five to ten minutes, to get myself ready, find the keys, and I will be with you soon.

Kathy got herself ready, and waited outside for Laura, watching every car go by, wondering which one was coming next, ten minutes later, Laura car was seen coming down the road towards Kathy's house.

Laura car, pulled up, next to Kathy.

Kathy walked over to the car, and bent down to see if it was Laura, before jumping in at the passenger's seat.

'Hello Kathy,' shouted Laura, leaning across the passenger seat, opening s the door for her,

'How are you?' she asked Kathy.

'Okay thanks,' lied Kathy, but she was feeling sorrowful, and depressed but having Laura here, made her feel slightly better.

Kathy was very pleased to be getting away from the house, the reminder of Wayne was something she was glad not to see reminders of Wayne, and to be alone thinking that life was not easy for her, when the children returned, and she was not alone, thinking about her Wayne.

Kathy got in the car and sat down next to Laura.

'Don't forget your seat belt., said Laura reminding her to use it.

Yes, thanks, said a grateful Kathy.

Kathy was relieved to see Laura, she felt safe with the knowledge that Laura was a happy and

smiley and a positive person which she needed; this was the first time she had Wayne away since marrying him.

Over the seven weeks of Wayne being away, Kathy was getting better with her cooking, making new dishes, cottage pies, with lean mince meat, fish pies, puddings trying a crème caramel, made with eggs and milk, with a caramel, made with burnt sugar.

Laura also showed Kathy how to use cooking apples, to making a crumble, a lemon meringue pie, and a milk blancmange.

Another attribute that Laura had, she was good at housekeeping, her Mother was a clever lady, who came from a large family, so money had to be counted and carefully used to budget and pay bills, thus showing Kathy her knowledge that her own mother had taught her about paying electricity, gas bills and council tax, this was easy for Laura, who should gone into helping younger people on saving, and budgeting.

Wayne had had the operation and was back with his cousin Louie and his wife Chloe, he was.

getting used to his new routine too, going for walks in the morning, and a few simple exercises in the afternoon Wayne made his phone calls in the evening to the Broome household just to make sure everything was okay, and getting his call before the children, went to bed.

Kathy looked forward to her talks telling Wayne, about what Laura had taught her.

Roland told his Dad, he had to walk to school, and wanted him home to mend the car, and

He missed his Mum's driving them to school.

Wayne was not interested in Roland, about wanted him back for driving the car, he was still having pain from his knee operation, and was annoyed with Roland for making such a fuss,

about the walks to school, when his walks were a painful and difficult for this normally simple task for Roland.

Molly told Dad about the walks to school, and that Mum is making lovely meals, her favourite being Crème caramel, made with milk, eggs and covered with a burnt sugar.

coating, explaining to him, how Mum has to burn the sugar in a saucepan to make it black or brown depending how clever she is.

Why does Kathy burn the sugar? That is stupid' Wayne sounded angry.

Molly said to Wayne, don't be silly Dad, she didn't do it on purpose.

'Then why do it, then, Wayne enquired.

'It says that in the recipe. Silly Daddy,' sighed Molly, her eyes looking up at the ceiling with her silly Dad!!

Kathy got used to her lessons with Laura, and the children got into a routine, with going to school with Mum, then coming home at quarter to four each day, glad to sit down, have a cup of tea before give the children, brown sandwiches made with tomatoes, and tuna and salad cream fillings.

Kathy was enjoying her lessons from Laura, making new meals, finding out about electricity.

and gas bills, council taxes, and other problems, like making sure that the children drank more water, than fizzy drinks, and made sure that they visited the dentist more regular than Wayne and Kathy did who had a lot of fillings.

The weeks pasted with the children enjoying their walks, and sleeping better, and feeling fresh, healthy, positive and feeling happier, with their walking, which was getting easier for both Roland and Molly, Laura suggested to Kathy, to make the walks more interesting by asking the children to spot different birds, flowers in another people garden, and if they looked down on the pavement to see if they can spot a bumble bee resting on there, and not to stamp on the poor thing, if he needed to be put on a flower to revive himself (sometimes they stop and rest for a few minutes before flying away)

The children are now more aware of their surroundings, and they looked up and down, carefully not walking into a lamppost, with their observations, they sometimes see a bird, that looked like a plane, which may have been a swallow or a swift. Molly was looking at the hedgerow as she was walking and spotted in the hedgerow a shining-coloured light, she ran across to look closer at this shining light.

'Mum! look 'she said Roland and Kathy.

They went to where Molly was looking.

'What is it mum? it looks like a rainbow,' exclaimed Molly, excitedly.

'Oh! No! not another rainbow, first the cake and now this,' moaned Kathy, wondering what was going on here.

Kathy did not know what this was, she did not take much interest in science at school.

'I should ask your teacher, when you get back to school,' She said.

'Oh, how exciting a rainbow in the hedge,' exclaimed Molly getting excited.

Then Roland glanced down on the pavement and noticed an object that looked like a large brown nut, on the pavement.

'What is this? Inquired Roland, picking up the acorn in his hand, and he is showing it to Kathy and Molly.

'Do not pick up things off the floor,' grumbled Kathy, crossly.

I think it is some sort of seed,' thought Molly, it looks like a conker, maybe it is a chestnut,'

Kathy looking closely at it.

'Hmm, I am not sure what it is, when we get home, I will ask Laura maybe she has an answer,' said Kathy, puzzled but what else will her children find again.

After they all arrived home, Kathy rang Laura, she asked her about this large object, and described it to her,'

Laura said 'it sounds like an acorn,'

Molly knew after Kathy told her,

'Mum, this will grow into an oak tree. We must plant it.' Suggested Molly.

' Yes, what a good idea, maybe Laura, will have a spare pot, we definitely haven't got any pots ourselves,' admitted Kathy, feeling excited at this new adventure, of growing a large oak tree from a small seed, her parents never gave Kathy and Kenny, any opportunities to grow any seed or plant, they didn't even know that potatoes came from out of the ground, only arrived in the shops by magic.

When Kathy went to see Laura that day, she asked her about a spare flowerpot.

Laura took Kathy into the garage, where Steve had a stack of pots, neatly placed on shelf.

'Now! Kathy which pot do you want, a big pot, and middle size pot or a small one, asked.

Laura waiting for an answer from Kathy.

'I will have a small pot,' she said.

When it gets bigger, you can borrow a larger pot, Kathy too' Laura said being helpful.

Laura took down two pots and handed it to Kathy.

'Thanks Laura,' smiled Kathy, clutching the pot, as if it was something very expensive and fragile.

She took it home, and found a trowel in Wayne's shed, amongst a spade and a rusty pair of shears.

Roland, Molly and Kathy, went into the garden, to a corner of a flower bed, which was strewn with weeds, they managed to shovel some earth from there, and scooped some soil into the pot, filled the pot up with soil, found a watering can, also from the shed, filled the can with water, poured water all over it, and then buried the acorn into pot of sodden watered earth.

They brought it into the house, placed on the windowsill in the kitchen, over the six weeks, that Wayne was away the acorn grew.

Molly when she was back at school, asked the teacher about the rainbow in the hedge row,

Miss Harris said it sounds like a dewdrop, which when it catches the light from the sun, It forms a prism, and that is the same as the rainbow in the sky, but in the hedgerow, she also mentioned that sometimes when, it rained on a cobweb, this will also have a rainbow effect too.

Now the walks were more interesting, Roland and Molly told their teachers, about what they saw on their walks to school, every day, and their friends also ask them questions about what they have come across that day too, it made the children at school, talk to Roland with a better understanding, and this gave Roland a lovely feeling of being in demand, from his class mates, and getting them keen on going on walks, with their parents.

All the teachers put out a nature table in their classrooms, so that the children could put on.

their tables different nature finds.

Each classroom had a variety of nature items on their tables, from owls' pellets, flowers, old used bird's nests (do not find these in nesting times) and empty snail shells, with a beautiful pattern of yellow and brown stripes on them.

Molly and Roland told their teachers about the acorn being in a pot.

One teacher said that when it is a bit bigger, bring it to school, and they will make a special place, in the woods and we can plant it so it can get bigger.

Each day Kathy was getting more positive and confident, with her lessons with Laura, and

enjoying the achievement in creating new and exciting dishes, and her health and her children were also benefiting from these healthy meals.

When Wayne returns the lessons with Laura will get less frequent.

But Laura expressed 'you can ring me, anytime with any questions about cooking.'

Kathy could not wait to try out her new dishes on Wayne, and hopes he might eventually stop drinking beer again.

Kathy has decided to say to Wayne, if he drinks again, the children will be walking to school, and they will probably never go in the car or van, if you have been drinking that night, in fact Kathy wants to continue to walk, as now she does not need a sleep in the afternoon, as

Wayne has been away, letting Kathy catch up on her sleep, she is now more energised and happier.

After seven weeks away Wayne came back, very thin and different.

While Wayne was away his meals, Chloe has cooked were mostly vegetarians, she gave him less meat, lots of fruit, nuts and vegetables, and Louie gave Wayne lots of exercises.

Wayne used to go on walks, just to get away from the house, and Louie who was keen on

Wayne to do some indoor exercises, but walking was another exercise, that Louie was happy With Wayne doing any walking ....

This made Wayne miss his family even more, but he wanted to get back to his family, when he was able to.

He was used to being away from his home, when he was a young lorry driver, but he always knew he would get back eventually, unless he broke down, or he had to do more loads in his shift.

But now because of his bad knee, he could not come home easily, he now appreciated his

Home even more, he is now more passionate about life, his cousin is a fair man, and gave.

Wayne support about his bad life style, that he was used to having, as they are a fit couple they found Wayne a big challenge.

Eventually Wayne started to like his new way of living, his walking and being without his smoking, he could now appreciate the smell the fresh air, and knew that his cousin was not a bad person.

Louie hoped that Wayne would not go back to smoking and drinking again, and now Wayne was enjoying the healthy drinks that Chloe made for him, using fresh fruit and vegetables.

Wayne had also started to enjoy gardening, that had to be done, but as he had a knee.

replacement, they did not expect him to do too much,

but just pick fruit from the apple and pear trees.

He also had a lot of time, to think about what was more important to him, he realised that if he did not change his habits of drinking, and eating fatty meals, and occasionally smoking a cigarette or two, or going to the pub with Bill his mates, he could have ended up with a more serious illness or something worse. Cousin Louie, and his wife Chloe had a very healthy lifestyle, and at the beginning, this was something that frightened Wayne, making him panic, not to be able have a drink when he wanted one or have one cigarette when he was stressed.

Louie was very strict, with him, but in the end, Wayne got used to this way of life, eating a good vegetarian diet, and walking outside in the fresh air, because he had lost so much weight, he was looking younger, and was achieving more energy, and sleeping without the loud snore, that Kathy had to put up with, making Kathy sleep downstairs on the sofa, to avoid his snoring.

His clothes were starting to get loose, and he could not go out for walks, without his trousers falling down, he needed to get himself some new clothes. Louie took Wayne into town, and they took him to a good shop for men's outfits.

Louie saw that Wayne, had lost weight, and we wanted to treat him, to some new clothes for being a good patient.' Said Louie admiring him.

Wayne was very self-conscious in buying clothes in front of his cousin and Chloe, he was shown into the shop by Terence Sharp, he is a tall gentleman, very dapper, with a grey pinstripe suit, white shirt, a black tie covered with white spots dotted all over the tie.

Terence was very helpful, in putting Wayne at ease, giving him a good chair, then to be shown by Terence some outfits, while Louie and Chloe sat in another room, chatting,

Eventually Wayne had decided after Terence shown him some trousers, shirts, and jumpers rather than full matching suit and trousers, he decided on casual trousers, a pattern shirt, and a brown jumper.

He went out of the fitting room, and came in to show Louie and Chloe, his new outfit.

'Lovely, give us a twirl. I love it, how do you feel Wayne,' she asked smiling and pleased with the choice.

'Slim and comfortable,' admitted Wayne modestly.

By showing Terence by holding out his stretched arms, how much fatter he was.

'Yes! even now my new knee is feeling better, I can now run a marathon, bragged Wayne, jumping up from his chair and pretending to run.

Terence smiled nervously watching Wayne, pretending to run, he was worried that Wayne was going to fall over.

'Would, Sir, come this way sir,' asked Terence, walking towards a row of trousers, on the clothes rack.

'Now sir, what colour would you like,' asked Terence, eyeing Wayne, up and down.

'Dark Grey, maybe! Admitted Wayne, moving the trousers, and feeling the clothe as he was moving the trousers along the rack.

.' I like these,' announced, Wayne, pulling out the required trousers.

'Let me take your measurements, Terence said pulling off, the tape measure from his neck.

Terence ran the tape measure down Wayne's inside leg, right now your waist, he tied the tape measure, around Wayne's thin waist.

'Hmm, 36 inches around the waist, and 34 inches for his trousers, wait a minute while I find your size trousers.

Terence came back and showed the trousers, holding the against Wayne waist.

'Go and try them on sir, then you can walk up and down, with them on, to show your cousin them,' announced Terence watching Wayne.

Wayne came out of the changing room, and walked up and down, feeling slightly embarrassed, this is not a Wayne thing, to show off.

(If he saw a young man parading himself would, not say nice things about him, possibly showing off.)

Wayne found a lovely shirt, a coat, and a smart tie, all matched with all his grey outfit.

'Thank you, Terence, smiled Chloe.

'Yes! thank you, said Wayne, giving him a rough handshake.

They all left the shop, and got in the car parked, which was near the shops, and returned to

Their house, after coming into the house, Louie piped up, now he is an adult, we have done all, that we can for him, he needs to be at home back with his family, Kathy told me confidently, that she had now, had a good training for healthier diet from help from her good friend Laura, and now she will do her best, in keeping him well, if he puts on weight again, or smokes or drinks in excess, he will have to go back, to his old tatty clothes, and not his new ones, because they won't fit him, in fact he must keep slim another wise, Kathy will be angry, and walk out of him.

The next day Wayne was ready with his suitcase, at the door of Louie and Chloe house, ready and wanting to go home.

'Come on Wayne,' said Louie picking up his suitcase, Chloe, put Wayne's suitcase in the boot, and they jumped int the car, Chloe sat next to Louie in the passenger seat, and Wayne sat at the back. They drove off to Kathy's and Wayne's house.

They eventually arrived, back at Wayne house, with Kathy and Molly, who were watching out, from their front room window for their father to come home.

Molly, stood at the front window, watching out for her father, he was due back at four, in the afternoon.

Molly suddenly saw the car, coming down the road,

Mum, Mum! dad is coming,' shouted Molly, getting really excited at the prospect, of seeing her Dad again...

Kathy came over to Molly, who was trying to keep herself busy, waiting for Wayne, she decided to disappear in the kitchen and make some healthy snacks for Wayne. Kathy was very nervous of the prospect of having Wayne back, she felt after a long period of being alone, had made her independent and secure, with a knowledge of Laura's help in managing alone, she was worried about having a bossy husband again, she stood next to Molly at the window.

The car pulled up, Wayne got out of the car, and stepped out onto the pavement, Louie got out and opened the boot of the car, and dropped the suitcase, on the pavement, Wayne looked at his house, and saw Kathy and Molly at the window, waving frantically at him, they both rushed to the door and went out to greet them.

Wayne looked thin, but strangely handsome, in his new clothes, Chloe just stood there watching Wayne with his family, Louie, patted Wayne shoulders.

Molly stood with Kathy staring at her Dad, rather shy, and thinking, this is not my Daddy, he is thin and handsome.

Kathy thought she better pick up, Wayne's suitcase, the case was small and light, just an overnight case, for his overnight stay in Hospital, she was happy, but worried at her husband's thin appearance.

CHAPTER 13
AN ACORN, A RAINBOW AND A BABY OAK TREE

In the Broome household, Molly came down the stairs, as she did every day, examining the growing acorn, which was now in a bigger pot as it had grown too big for the small flowerpot one, it originally came in, it was on the shelf, but the shoot had grown much taller. She takes the pot plant down from the shelf and takes it into the kitchen where she finds Kathy.

'Mum, the acorn has grown much taller, can we take the oak plant, to school today,' enquired Molly.

Molly had put the pot on the kitchen table.

Molly, sitting down for breakfast.

'Okay, we will, right away, but we need to get it there safely, or we may break the plant, but as Roland found it first, it only fair that Roland must carry it, and explain to Mrs Saunders that he found it on the pavement,' explained Kathy.

Roland who was also in the kitchen, overheard the conversation about the acorn.

'Mum, can carry it, said Roland, glad someone else can carry this awkward plant.

Kathy went to the drawer to find some brown paper, from the kitchen drawers, where she keeps, her wrapping paper, and foil.

Kathy carefully takes the plant from the pot, and she carefully wraps, it with brown paper.

'This is exciting,' cried Molly, grinning with excitement, who was more excited than Roland, who was happy just leaving the acorn on the pavement, he hated all this fuss over a silly acorn.

Kathy, Molly, and Roland all set off to School, with Kathy, carefully carrying, the fragile shoot in the brown bag, to school.

Molly walked, feeling proud, they had grown an oak tree!!!

Roland followed behind them, he was glad it was in Kathy's hands and not his, Molly was excited about the plant more than he was, so if he broke the stem, it would be Molly moaning at him for being so clumsy.

Finally, they arrived at their school, as they wanted to arrive early, so the children, could accompany Kathy, to the headmistress's room, before their class started.

'Where is Mrs Saunders's room, Molly? asks Kathy.

'Follow me, informed Molly, cheerfully.

Roland and Kathy followed Molly up some stairs, and along the corridor, and eventually arrived at the door saying, THE HEADMISTRESSES ROOM, written, on an oak brown plaque.

They all stood outside the room, with Kathy clutching the brown package, containing the acorn shoot.

Kathy looked at the two children and said 'Right you two, I will knock, and I hope, Mrs Saunders is in there.

Kathy knocked nervously on the door.

'Yes, come in,' answered Mrs Saunders.

Kath walked in first, and produced the tree, to Mrs

Saunders, she plonked it gently, on her oak table desk.

'Kathy explained, 'We found an acorn, on the pavement as we were walking to school, so, we took it home and planted it in a pot, and now we are hoping, that maybe, Mrs Saunders, you could plant the tree, in your school woods, and hopefully, it will grow into a good tree, and maybe you will have a tree, that your next, future children can enjoy.

'Oh, lovely, said, Mrs Saunders, sounding very pleased and excited.

' I will go, and ask Jeff, our caretaker, to find a good spot, to plant your oak tree, how exciting our first oak tree, grown from an acorn, by one of our pupils,' says Mrs Saunders clapping her hands with glee.

Adding, 'I will arrange for your two classes, Roland and Molly, to watch me plant it, if you just wait here, I will just go, and find the caretaker, and ask him to produce a spade, for this task,' announced Mrs Saunders.

She left her room, while Kathy and the children, were still amazed at Mrs Saunders's responsive reaction, to their tree, and getting this done, straight away.

Mrs Saunders walked over to the caretaker's hut.

'Jeff, are you in your shed,' she shouted,

'Yes, I am in here answered back promptly, he came outside to find Mrs Saunders, standing there grinning.

'Could you find a spot for an oak tree, one of our children, had grown an oak tree, from an acorn, they found it on the pavement, so we need a place in our woods, for the young tree, to grow into a tree,' asked Mrs Saunders.

'Yes, Missy Saunders, right away,' he replied.

'I will go back, and tell the Broome family the good news,' announced Mrs Saunders.

She quickly walked, back to the school, and came back into her room, where the family were all waiting anxiously, that he would have a spade.

'Jeff, said, he would get a plot ready, for the tree, and he would dig a large hole to put the tree obviously, this will take a long time to grow, into a strong and tall tree, and then it will produce more acorns, which in turn will grow more oak trees, maybe one day, the children of this school, may even climb this tree, with care,' admitted Mrs Saunders.

Kathy asked Mrs Saunders, 'Where are you going, to put the shoot in the meanwhile? worried it would wither and dry up before reaching the woods.

'Leave it with me, we can put it in a vase ready, when he has found a space for this plant. explained Mrs Saunders.

Kathy left the school and went back home, the children returned to their classrooms.

That afternoon Mrs Saunders took Roland and Mollie's classes, to an area of the school grounds where, Jeff, had found a special spot, to plant the tree, he informed Mrs Saunders.

Mrs Saunders went over to meet Jeff, who was in his shed, waiting for Mrs Saunders to appear.

'We are ready Jeff,' Mrs Saunders announced.

'I have found a good spot for the tree already, it is on the outskirts of the wood,' Mrs Saunders informs Jeff, getting his spade from the shed.

They both walked over, to the woods, where the two

classes had located, with forty or more children, chatting and laughing, at this new venture, who were in awe of this ceremony, to take place in the dark woods of the school.

Jeff gave Mrs Saunders the spade and then showed Mrs Saunders the area where he had dug a hole for the tree.

'Here is the spot for your plant,' informs Jeff, standing over the area.

Mrs Saunders promptly put the tree in the hole.

Roland, stood watching this being done,

'Can I put some earth on the plant,' he asked.

Yes,' of course, and Molly can too,' admitted Mrs Saunders,

Now Roland, here is the spade, he came over, and scooped.

'Now it is your turn, Molly' says Mrs Saunders.

Molly went over to where Roland was standing, Roland handed the spade over to Molly, she took it and thanked Roland.

She shovelled some earth, from the same pile of earth as Roland did, near the spade, and threw the earth down a hole, next to the tree.

'Thank you, Molly and Roland,' grinned Mrs Saunders gratefully, she trod down on the earth, with her lace-up thick brown shoes, making them compact, and tidy, Jeff butted in, 'I will give it a bucket of water, to help it grow strong and healthy, until it manages on its own,' announced Jeff.

All the children clapped with joy.

' Thank you, Roland and Molly, we may have more

oak trees, appearing now, other children are also, taking part in growing acorns in pots, so we may even get given a beech tree, a sycamore tree, or even a horse chestnut tree, full of conkers to play with, that is when they find any smaller seeds to plant it with,' hopefully announces Mrs Saunders,

Several weeks later the tree in the woods, has kept growing, much to the delight of the Broome family.

Molly and Roland felt very important having the first tree, to be planted on the school grounds.

Some of the children even came to the school, and peered through the school bar railing, on their school holidays to see how well it was growing, although the school grounds, were locked in safety reasons, they could still peep through the railings, to see it growing, and if it is safe, from animals, scratching the tree.

Mrs Coates, decided to make a tapestry picture of an acorn, growing into a tree, and she proudly put her framed picture on the wall, of the school hallway, underneath the picture the words made with light green thread, "SMALL STEPS ARE THE BEGINNING OF BIGGER STEPS, which everyone who ever you are can change for the better, but you need to take it slowly and, in the end, will be proud of what you have achieved.

The Broome family are a good example of change, Wayne has now decided that his bad knee was the start of a wakeup call, and something had to change, his cousin has given him a hard time away, making him go without all the things in his life that help him cope with life at home, which were bad for his health. But he decided to stay a few more weeks until as Louie said he could touch his toes, and walk upstairs without being puffed out, which was a good healthy sign.

Kathy had also found Wayne had changed, for the better. After seven weeks of being away, Wayne had come back, very different and somehow more handsome, in fact, she was wondering if he was going to be a more considerate and affectionate man, which before he was selfish, greedy, and grumpy.

One Saturday Wayne left the house before Kathy had realised; he had gone.

Kathy was alone in the kitchen, and the children were somewhere in the house.

Wayne had not asked for a drink or something to eat, and wondered where he was, was he ill? And gone out and forgetting where he lived?

Wayne had been home a few weeks, but never left the house, since Kathy had taken the children to school leaving Wayne back home on his own,

Soon he was going get back to his job, but only pastime until he was fully fit and going back full time.

Twenty minutes later Wayne returned back home.

Kathy was busy in the kitchen preparing some healthy drinks for the children when Wayne came into the kitchen, Kathy had her back to Wayne at that moment.

'Kathy,' whispered Wayne.

'Turn around I want to see you facing me,' he asked kindly.

Kathy turned around, and then Wayne walked over to Kathy and pushed a bunch of flowers into Kathy's hands.

'What is this, Wayne? did you find them outside on the pavement,' she asked embarrassed to receive these flowers that Wayne had given her.

'I wanted to give you these flowers for putting up with me, for all these few years, I have been a bad person taking you for granted, and you have kept the family going despite me being away with my cousin Louie and Chloe, they both made me better, and they have put up with me, despite sometimes I have been very grumpy, and they have said nothing, but walked away for me to simmer down alone, and I now realise that I have been grumpy to you sometimes, and you have put up with me, that is all,' said Wayne, he then walked away embarrassed to what he just said, after his long speech. He felt red with such a long speech, which he never usually said to Kathy before,

Kathy stood flabbergasted at Wayne's emotional speech, a slight tear filled her eyes, and she wiped it away quickly.

When she had got herself composed again, she looked at her flowers and realised that amongst the flowers were some red roses, these are signs of love, that is so nice to think of me.

And though I must put these in a vase quickly, I have no vase.

Kathy looked in a cupboard to see if she could see anything possible to put them in a large old cup, or container, and suddenly noticed at the bottom of the cupboard a vase, where did that come from? She thought very puzzled.

'Oh! Of course, Laura gave me a present on my birthday, when she was helping me with these meals, I completely forgot about it.

Kathy filled the vase up with water, and walked into the sitting room, proudly carrying the vase, and promptly putting it on the windowsill.

Molly was sat there watching television, and Roland was in the bathroom.

Wayne saw Kathy come into the sitting room carrying the vase with the flowers in it, walking into the sitting room, after having felt embarrassed at his long speech and not saying it before.

The rest of the evening was strange but happy.

Kathy kept this feeling of power now, and Wayne was quieter but they both realised that life was going to maybe change for the better.

Wayne was kinder to the children and thought he would take the children one day, to the park, and surprise the Silverton children, his children may find them, and Sammy and Sally could teach them how to play in the woods.

CHAPTER 14
MR QUICK THE BANK MANAGER

Laura has suggested to Kathy, that her children need pocket money every week, just a small amount, she said that Sammy and Sally are using their banks to save their money.

Kathy went along to Laura's bank, to be introduced to her bank manager.

After the meeting, Kathy took Molly and Roland to the bank, and while they were there, they were asked to go into his office.

After a long talk with all of them, Mr Quick left them alone, while he went to get two piggy banks for the children. Mr Quick the bank manager said that when they get to sixteen years old, they will have a Saving account, and a paying-in book, to use when depositing money, making them feel grown up and important, in the meantime, Mr Quick suggested they have a piggy bank, he gives a piggy bank in the shape of an acorn, and eventually an account called an oak account.

Before they left the office, Mr Quick gave Kathy his card.

'Thank you,' replied Kathy.

She glanced down at the card, and it said Mr B. Quick the Bank Manager.

Kathy showed the card to the children, they thought that was a good name, considering the bank manager left the office quickly coming back as quickly as his name.

Roland is now saving up fast for a new bicycle, with the help of saving with hi new piggy Bank. A piggy bank is something that Kathy had never given them, to save their money in,

The bank manager explained to Kathy, that this was the way children would enjoy the excitement of achieving an item, that they had saved up, and bought with themselves,

Kathy had not been able to afford big toys before, but this way they know that they will get one, but it does take time, and the more they work they do the quicker they will get their toys.

The children love their new piggy banks, and when they save more, they will get an Oak Account because they have reached the one-hundred-pound mark with their new amount in this account, young children can have the rainbow-coloured piggy bank, with a pink background.

Their new account is the Acorn account, and the Rainbow account, both for young people.

The difference is the books are different, but the accounts are the same, with their new piggy banks, the money is being carefully monitored not to be wasted, Roland has thought of ways to earn some more pocket money, by cutting people lawns, there are a few older neighbours who are glad of a young person to do it, Roland loves the older neighbours, they give him lemonade and biscuit, but Roland is good he only has one, and Molly is also doing some more jobs, she has offered to take people dogs for a walk, which is a great help to some of the older people who are bored with this exercise the neighbours do the morning walk and Molly does the evening walk, both Roland and Molly are also keeping fit with their jobs, Roland has his eye on a red one, and Molly wanted a prettier one than Roland, she has a few choices to choose from.

Sammy and Sally continue playing in the park, they think that they are just happy there and have discovered that someone has tied a thick long rope to a tree, which they are secretly going to play with and enjoying swinging to and fro.

In the woods, which are for finding out, about many exciting discoveries, they came across a toadstool which looked very magical, with red spots on top of it, they thought maybe it was connected to the fairies, but they did not see any fairies there yet!! They often see squirrels, and grey rabbits have also appeared there too, Sally has found beautiful red and orange leaves, which they have taken back home, and amongst the leaves have found some acorns, which they may plant in pots, and they can add to Roland and Mollies oak tree one day soon.

About the Author

The Author is born and educated in Newton Abbot, Devon. Now single and pursuing a new venture of creative arts. This quiet hobby takes her to exciting places with her imagination to write these stories came about.